THE
PURPOSE
BEHIND
THE PAIN

The remarkable sequel to Waiting On God...Fear Is Not An Option

JASON B. HENRY

Order this book online at www.trafford.com
or email orders@trafford.com

Most Trafford titles are also available at major online book retailers.

Printed in the United States of America.

ISBN: 978-1-4669-8912-2 (sc)
ISBN: 978-1-4669-8911-5 (e)

Trafford rev. 05/24/2013

Trafford
PUBLISHING®   www.trafford.com

North America & international
toll-free: 1 888 232 4444 (USA & Canada)
phone: 250 383 6864 ♦ fax: 812 355 4082

Contents

In Loving Memory of Genevieve Costello
1987-2013

Acknowledgments

This book is dedicated to our Lord and Savior Jesus Christ Almighty. Thank you for choosing me as the "man for the job." I never saw this coming, but I welcome the challenge! I waited patiently and You healed me. I will always share with others about Your goodness and let the world know that You are real. Please continue to show me direction in other areas of my life. Lord, I love You!

A special thank you to my parents:

Mom, I really appreciate the countless hours you spent once again assisting with the editing of the material for this book. Dad, thank you for always being there for me. I could not have done any of this without you both.

To Jerry, Howard and Mike, thank you guys for being the most amazing brothers anyone could ever ask for.

Thank you to my family for your prayers and support. I love you all.

Thank you to Granny Rogers and all my aunts and uncles—you all have been instrumental in my healing process.

Thank you to my prayer warriors:

Pastor Via Mosby and the Miraculous Ministries congregation—
—We fought the devil together!

Bishop Kenneth Ulmer and First Lady Tee—Faithful Central Bible Church

Pastor King Dale and Lady V. Renee Felton—More Sure Word Training Center

Thank you to my very special medical team:

Dr. Pearl Evelyn Grimes, World Renowned Dermatologist, Melea Futrell and the Vitiligo Pigmentation Institute staff—You all are truly a blessing. Keep doing what you're doing.

To my special friend, Resheida—thank you for being that friend I needed to help me get through my most difficult time.

To Ms. Brady, Denise, Loretta, Latanya, Michelle J., Andre, Darlyn, Porshea, Josh, Brandyn C., Greg—thank you all for always keeping in touch and checking in on me.

Book Project/Editing: Sonia Henry & Alex Schnitzler, Editing Consultant.

Introduction

They say life is a journey, and so far mine has been nothing short of amazing. It is true that it hasn't always been easy for me, but through it all, I have grown and learned so much about myself and about others, and how to live my best life while dealing with adversities. I quickly learned that hanging my head and feeling sorry for myself was not the answer. That was not making things any better. Instead, I learned how to make lemonade when life gave me lemons. While my story has been an inspiration to many, I continue to strive to do what I believe God has intended for my life, and that is to serve Him and to help others to get to know Him.

Since May 2010, I have been living with a rare and incurable scalp condition, Perifolliculitis Capitis Abscedens et Suffodiens. Having gone from doctor to doctor, trying the many treatment plans they recommended, trying other remedies such as herbs, cleanses, Chinese medicine and acupuncture, and since the release of *Waiting on God* in October 2011, my family and I continued our search for answers and for a healing. On this journey, I have grown so much spiritually and have developed a personal relationship with my Lord and Savior, Jesus Christ. While friends have come and gone, Jesus has always been my rock.

The Journey

It was just after my 23rd birthday when my life took me on a roller coaster ride after I was diagnosed with Perifolliculitis Capitis Abscedens et Suffodiens. Research shows it is a therapeutically challenging suppurative scalp disease of unknown etiology. It predominantly occurs in black males in their second-to-fourth decade of life. The most common age group affected is between ages 18-40 years. It is not life threatening, but the clinical course is chronic and unpredictable with relapses, although spontaneous resolution may occur. It is found mostly in men, although cases in women are also reported. Oral isotretinoin (Accutane) is the treatment of choice for this condition.

In layman's language, what started as a tiny bald spot, smaller than a dime, in the middle of my head, turned into large and very inflamed boils that spread all over my head and down the sides of my neck. I remember standing in front of the mirror, screaming in pain while blood clots oozed from the boils on my neck. They were extremely painful and leaked pus and blood almost constantly. My mom helped me with washing the bloody sheets, pillowcases and towels every day. Needless to say, besides having to cope with the pain, there was a lot of frustration, embarrassment and disappointments. I got very little sleep at night for about a year and a half because it was almost impossible to find a comfortable position to lay my head. Even the slightest touch of my head on the pillow would hurt really badly. As a result, I was always very tired and moody. I struggled through my days at work. In fact, it was so bad I could hardly function without pain medication. Eventually, the doctor put me off work for several months while we find a treatment plan that worked.

Because I was so embarrassed, everything I was going through was top secret. My immediate family, a few other family members and very close friends were the only people who knew what I was dealing with. My social life came to a complete halt as I had to wear a hat or some form of head covering whenever I was out in public, and most of the clubs had dress codes in place that did not allow hats so I stayed home. I was also afraid that while I tried to hide under the hats, something or someone would come along and cause the hat to fall and expose my big secret. As time went on, I was hearing from my friends less and I would only imagine the fun they were having without me. I felt like I was losing my friends. I didn't have a girlfriend and I often wondered if I would ever find one who would love me despite what I was going through. I felt so alone. The insecurities were mounting up and my self-esteem was at its lowest point. I tried really hard to stay strong for my family and friends, but I was angry with God and I questioned Him. Why God, why did you allow this to happen to me?

Thanksgiving Day 2011

The more accepting I became of this rare medical condition, the more I began to realize that through it all I was going to have to trust somebody. After all, it had been about a year and a half since this whole medical ordeal started, and I had been to several different doctors and tried many different medications, none of which seemed to work for too long before I had another flare-up. Needless to say, I just couldn't get enough of getting on my knees, praying and crying out to God and begging Him to have mercy on me and take it away.

For some odd reason, my family and I never went to church on Thanksgiving Day. It just seemed like Thanksgiving Day was about eating lots and lots of good food and then slipping into a food coma. We would, however, pray together and never forget to give God thanks for all of the things that we usually take for granted daily. Thanksgiving Day 2011 was different for me though. My friend, Resheida, invited me to go to church with her again and I promised her I would. As difficult as it was for me to drag myself out of bed that morning, everything in my spirit was telling me I needed to go. I quickly got dressed and met her there. Because we were running a little late, we quietly slipped into some seats at the back of the church. Resheida wanted to move up a little closer to where we normally sat, but I insisted that we stay right there in the back. Not too long after, I just happened to glance over to my right and saw a young man with a scalp condition that looked very similar to mine. His head was not covered, so for the entire service I just stared at his head. I felt like I was looking at myself and I just kept thinking, "Wow! Here is someone just like me. I know what he's going through. I wonder how he's coping?" The Pastor asked all first-time visitors to stand so that the congregation could welcome them, and the young man stood up. This was not a coincidence at all that this was happening.

I knew I had to talk to him after the service. I whispered to Resheida that I wished I had a copy of *Waiting on God: Fear is Not an Option*. To my surprise, she just happened to have her copy with her and she pulled it from her purse and gave it to me. That was such an unselfish thing for her to do. I was so happy about the way everything was working out. None of this was a coincidence—it was meant to happen this way. I could feel this young man's pain and I wanted him to be encouraged. I wanted him to know what his options are and I was hoping that he would choose Jesus, like I did. In my book I talked quite a bit about how I was coping with my own insecurities, fears, pain and discomfort from the condition. In it are also some encouraging words for anyone who may be dealing with something in their lives and don't know what to do or where to turn. "If only he could read my book and realize that he is not alone," I thought.

I approached the young man and introduced myself. I told him that I saw him in church and could not help but notice that we had something in common. We compared notes. He told me a little bit about what he had been dealing with and what course of treatment he was taking. His story pretty much mirrored mine, but he looked very sad. I gave him my book and explained that writing and sharing my story was good therapy for me. More importantly, it brought me closer to Jesus. I think meeting each other was good for both of us. It was my first time actually seeing and meeting someone else with the same condition. We exchanged contact information and said we would stay in touch. I was thankful that I had the opportunity to encourage someone else who may have needed it at that very moment. That was my best Thanksgiving Day ever.

Wrong Place, Perfect Timing

In November 2011, a friend referred me to a doctor whom she believed might be able to help me. It was perfect timing because, at that point, I had exhausted all my search options and was waiting on God to direct my next steps. We wasted no time in scheduling an appointment with the recommended doctor. On the day of the appointment, my mom decided she would go with me to the doctor. She always accompanied me to the medical appointments when I was seeing the doctors for the first time. She wanted to meet the doctors personally to discuss the condition, the treatments we had already tried, and to find out what their treatment plan would be.

As soon as we walked into the doctor's office, my mom whispered to me that she did not think we were at the right place; this doctor's specialty was treating the head and neck, not the skin. Nevertheless, since we were already there, we saw the doctor and he basically told us that there was nothing he could do for me, except to refer me to a good dermatologist. Again, we immediately jumped at the opportunity to do whatever we could to find a good treatment plan.

Good But Not Good Enough

For the next three months I treated with a very nice dermatologist in Beverly Hills, California. I could not have asked for a more gentle and caring doctor and her medical staff. The office environment was by far the best I had seen thus far. They worked really hard to find the best possible treatment for this skin condition that they had never seen or treated before. They even brought in doctors from the best major medical facilities in the state to get their input, but eventually they admitted that what they were doing was not working, and there was really nothing else they could do for me. They did, however, refer me to a facility they considered to be the best of the best, with a department that specialized in the treatment of skin disorders. By that time, I was getting very discouraged and running low on patience. I told my mom that would be the last dermatologist I was going to treat with. I was anxious to see what their new treatment plan would be. After all, everything I had tried so far worked only for a short time before my scalp would flare up again.

It had been almost two years since the beginning of this whole ordeal and my most of my co-workers had no idea what I was dealing with from day to day. The pain was no joke and the draining and bleeding were not getting any better. As a matter of fact, the situation had gone from bad to worse. Sometimes at work I took long bathroom breaks and just sat in the stall with a pool of blood on the floor from my scalp bleeding and dripping. I was too embarrassed to tell anyone about it. Nighttime was the worse; I got very little sleep, as it was hard to get my head in a comfortable position on the pillow. The situation had become almost unbearable, but I tried to be strong. Enjoying a social life was definitely a thing of the past.

Could This Be The Answer To My Prayers?

It was a nice and sunny morning in March 2012 when I walked into the new dermatologist's office overwhelmed with excitement. According to our research, the doctor I was about to see was the head of the dermatology department and she specialized in exactly the same skin condition I am dealing with. Yes! What more could I ask for? I was so ready to start a treatment plan that would work. My mom and brother, Mike, went with me to the appointment. We were all excited, but not for long. The doctor was not very pleasant, not compassionate, and had a very nonchalant attitude throughout the entire office visit. She answered all our questions though, indicating that she had seen various stages of the condition; mine, she said, was among the most severe. Nevertheless, her treatment plan was no different from all the other doctors I had seen. It was always a few different kinds of antibiotics, along with topical treatments and Vitamin A supplements. All that was bad news for me. I was frustrated and I felt like I was at the end of my rope.

I was only willing to try this doctor's treatment for about three months. After all, that's how long she said it would take, after starting the medications, before we would see any results. So I told myself I wasn't going to waste my time seeing her any longer than I needed to. Because the pain, swelling, and drainage had become so bad, she recommended that I take some time off from work to rest and take care of myself. It was such a relief not having to go to work while dealing with all the embarrassment, pain and discomfort.

Two months passed and it looked like these new medications were not working either. All the dermatologists I had seen so far had very similar treatment plans that seemed to work for a short while but did nothing for the healing of the skin. It became obvious that it was time for an alternative plan. Several friends and family members had been recommending that I try some homemade remedies, including swimming at the beach every day so that my head could get soaked in the salty water, and drinking a mixture of special herbs prepared by a "bush" doctor who said he grew up in the jungles of Belize and learned from his father about the healing properties of different herbs. I was up for the challenge. I asked myself, "What have I got to lose?" But after about one month of drinking the herbs, my scalp only got worse and I had to discontinue that plan. Staying in church and praying and crying out to God was all I had left.

A Divine Set Up

Because I felt the need to wear a hat at all times, and because of my prior experience at another church who had a "no hats" policy for men, which I talked a little bit about in *Waiting On God*, I was a little reluctant to go to church with Resheida on Sundays. However, the very first time I went with her, she introduced me to the pastor and explained to him my health issues and the reason for the hats. The pastor told me that he was personally extending an invitation to me to feel free to come to services whenever I wanted to, and that it was okay for me to wear hats. I immediately felt very comfortable and welcomed there. I finally felt like I had found a home church.

One Sunday morning in May 2012, we greeted the pastor after church service and he asked Resheida to give him a call later on that day because he wanted to give her the name of a very good dermatologist, a friend of his, whom he thought might be able to help me. Of course, my first thoughts were, "here we go again, another dermatologist!" But when we got the doctor's information, I realized that the pastor was recommending the same doctor whom my sister-in-law, Jeni, had told me about previously. Although, about a year ago when Jeni recommended the doctor and I did some research, I found out that the doctor did not, at the time, accept the insurance I had. Hearing about the doctor for the second time though really sparked some interest in us so my mom looked her up again. We wasted no time scheduling an appointment when we found out that she was now accepting my insurance!

In June 2012 my mom and brother, Mike, went with me to my first appointment with this new dermatologist. It was a very emotional visit for all of us. I think that was because we were expecting so little, but left the doctor's office that day feeling like she really and truly cared about me and wanted to help. She talked to my mom from a doctor's standpoint then talked to her from a mother's standpoint. Not very many doctors will do that. Making that personal connection with her gave us lots of hope. She was very straightforward and very confident about her treatment plan. She explained that the doses of medications that the previous doctors had prescribed were definitely not enough to fight this condition. She also explained that because there was so much infection, she was going to have to take a very aggressive approach. Mom was, undoubtedly, very scared about the side effects of all the medications I had been taking, and more so now, what I was going to have to take. Nevertheless, the doctor begged my mom, "please, let me help your son!" With our permission, she wasted no time putting her treatment plan into effect that very day. She had almost all of her staff rallying around me to make sure we were off to a good start.

I was tired and frustrated and ready for this thing to go away so I was willing to try this more aggressive approach, including the dreaded medication, Accutane, which I swore I would never take. I had no choice but to trust God for His protection, and I did a lot of praying about it. Mom said she prayed and prayed a lot too about all of the medications. She asked God to protect me from their harmful side effects and said she was comforted by a small voice that spoke to her and said, "don't be afraid." She believed that was God telling her that He's got my back. I am His child and His love is unfailing.

It was no more than a week after I started treating with this new doctor that the pain had subsided tremendously. I cannot tell you how excited I was to be able to get some sleep again. For five to six months I visited the doctor once a week, then in January 2013, I started seeing her twice a month. I am now off of the Accutane, and the doses for the other medications have been decreasing slowly. Thanks to the doctor, her aggressive approach worked and I am happy to say that today I am completely pain free. My scalp is almost completely flat—no more lumps or bumps, except for the occasional small flare-ups that are easier for the doctor to treat. In fact, at my last visit to the doctor, she explained that the areas that are not completely flat are mostly just scar tissues. Needless to say,

I have been jumping up and down thanking and praising God like I have never done before! Unlike those times when I didn't want anyone or anything to come near me for fear of them touching my head, even slightly, I am now able to hit my head with my hands to show my family there is no more pain.

In all my prayers and praising and thanking God, I asked Him for a healing and promised Him that if He healed me, I would NEVER stop talking about Him. I used to be the kid who never liked praying, or reading the Bible, or going to church. Even when I struggled with difficult situations, God was always my last resort, until this scalp disease brought me to my knees. Words cannot express how thankful I was that Jesus was there the whole time, waiting for me to call on Him.

The Richness of Family And Friends

The support I got from family members and friends has been nothing short of astonishing, especially from those closest to me. Usually when a friend or loved one has a financial need, or another need of some sort, helping them out with some money or whatever it is that they are needing usually takes care of the problem. However, when a loved one is suffering with pain and discomfort, there is always that feeling of helplessness, and the best thing that you or anyone can do for them is to just be there in whatever way you can. In my situation, other than showering me with comforting words, the only thing my family could do was to pray with me and for me. Mike wrote me a very lengthy letter during my difficult time, reminding me that God did not give me this scalp disease. In fact, He is not only ready to heal but to restore me. It is true that all things work together for good, and that sometimes God allows us to go through some situations in order that He can teach us and build our characters. God uses our times of adversities as opportunities to reveal Himself because He wants the glory. ". . . For I know the plans I have for you, declares the Lord, plans to prosper you and not to harm you, plans to give you hope and a future." (Jeremiah 29:11)

Jerry's Letter

My brother, Jerry, shared with the family that one day while he was feeling helpless about my situation, he wrote a letter to God, questioning Him as to why He allowed this to happen to his little brother, me. This is what he wrote:

> *Dear God,*
>
> *I just wanted to speak to you for a minute about Jason. I was just wondering why you did this to him. I thought that was pretty messed up. How would you like this stuff on your head or your body? I figured since you had already caught me by surprise with all my health issues and mistakes in 2006, it would have been easier if you would have just let me have this one too, since I am already probably strong enough to handle it. So, why did you choose Jason? Why not Howard or Mike, one of the other brothers?*
>
> *God: Jerry, you wouldn't quite understand, but I will try to explain since you asked.*
>
> *Jerry: Ok!*
>
> *God: As you know, your brother, Howard, has been in the biggest test of his life. There are many parts to his test, with a few trick questions about*

his own young family; multiple choice, some essay questions, a lot of critical reasoning. I think he is going to pass though. As for your brother, Mike, he is a tricky one. He knew his test was coming so he got real close to me, like a disciple. He likes to pray and write prayers and he has been writing for a while, but I am not sure what it is about yet. He even has a separate bank account for his tithes. I think he was trying to test me even. He has actually been waiting on me for a while. Don't worry; his test is not over yet. For now, if it makes you happy, Jerry, I will give him really bushy eyebrows and tiny feet. Oh, and did you notice he can make really, really good music, but he can't dance a lick. Anyway, what is happening to Jason was meant to make him stronger and take him one step closer to being a responsible man who can look within himself for strength, and find me when he feels alone and hopeless.

Jerry: I'm listening . . .

God: I didn't choose his head and the medical condition; I chose the lesson for him. But since you asked how I would feel if it were on my face or on my body, I would entertain that . . .

Jerry: Be my guest, you're the Lord, weren't you going to do it anyway?

God: Yes, so sit down and take note.

Jerry: I'm ready!

God: What do you think I am experiencing when there is a major earthquake, or viral outbreak, or violent massacre of people in this world I created?

Do you not think those are horrible sores on the 'body' of work I created? And what do you think about those floods and Tsunamis that wipe out thousands of people at once? Or, when people fly airplanes into buildings and families burn into memories? Doesn't it all seem painful?

Jerry: Well, yeah . . . of course!

God: And what do people do then?

Jerry: I don't know . . . get worried, scared, cry, and beg for mercy?

God: Not quite what I was getting at.

Jerry: Help me then!

God: Well, people have to rally around one another, strengthen their faith, and increase their hope. They have to make a conscious decision to rally around one another and lean each other and on family and come find me, even though they may not see me or feel me. Get it? They have to accept what it is. Or, in other words, that I am sure you have heard . . . many are called, but few have been chosen . . .

Jerry: I feel where you are coming from. I didn't think of it that deeply. But how long will this last with Jason?

God: As long as it needs to.

Jerry: I can see where this process has begun to change Jason. He wrote a book about it you know?

God: Uh, yeah. Thanks, but I kind of knew this already. So, when his levies break and his tears flood, YOU be there to wipe them! When he can't bear the weight, YOU lift it! When he feels like no one understands, YOU understand! When he runs out of patience, YOU be patient for him! When his pockets dry up searching for cures, YOU fill them! Didn't you help to change his diapers, make his bottles, and brush his teeth? And didn't you and Howard teach him how to walk?

Jerry: Yes, Sir.

God: Now show him how to live! Now back to you, mister inquisitive.

Jerry: Me?

God: Yes!

Jerry: Lets not, I get the point.

God: No, let's! So, in 2006, the eye surgeries, the heart surgery, the bad business situations . . . loss of money, loss of friends you thought were friends . . . those were all lessons. You finally reached the bottom when you stopped digging. You knew something was happening to you. You ran around to everyone saying, "Something is happening to me!" You were on to something. Didn't I give you clear visions? What was the title of Bishop's service that same weekend?

Jerry: "Something's Happening to Me!"

God: Right! You thought that guy you were doing business with at the time had something to do with that? No, that was I talking directly to you! Do you feel foolish yet?

Jerry: Not yet . . . I graduated. Just kidding. I don't feel very wise all of a sudden.

God: Weren't you scared? Weak? Insecure? You couldn't even see with your own eyes!!! You were in positions where you felt no one could help you, huh? You didn't have a job and you certainly were not the breadwinner.

Jerry: Yeah.

God: So whom did you turn to?

Jerry: Mom and Dad, and YOU!

God: and Howard, and Jason, and Mike. I heard every prayer and counted all the tears you cried in private. I was the only one at all the private pep rallies you had for yourself while driving to work. And yes, you did look sort of crazy to the other people in traffic, but that's ok. It was funny.

Jerry: True.

God: So why not you, you asked? 'Cause you have been working through your own tests. Don't fail now . . . and don't give up on God . . . He is able!

Jerry: Why are you bragging?

God: Because we can!

Jerry: We? Who are "we"?

God: I have a Son of my own, you know?

Jerry: Go ahead and show off then!

God: Well, since you doubted me and questioned me, I figured I wouldn't give you that house on the hill since you have a foreclosure on your record. Your wife wasn't even working at the time, so why would I even put that pressure on you guys. I won't help you get into your dream job and her get into hers. I won't fill your rental houses with loving tenants. In fact,

I will keep you in debt, your cars won't be paid off, and you won't even make it to five years of marriage. And that heart of yours that was slowly running out of beats . . . I won't bother to fix that either. As for your parents, you always worried about me taking them way too soon. Vacations to relax, forget about it! And I know you've been asking for a baby boy, but it will most likely be a girl! Why don't you look around your life and see where I am?

Jerry: I get it.

God: You're sure? Don't worry about Jason. I got HIM! At least he listened. He finished a book. Didn't I also inspire you to write a book?

Jerry: Yes, but . . .

God: Why is it only halfway done?

Jerry: It was hard at that one part . . .

God: Go bless someone in need. You already put your life in my hands, so I put my hands on your life.

Jerry: I see. Well, would you mind continuing to watch over us all? We need that.

God: Done!

Jerry: Thank you, Jesus. Glory be to God! Amen.

I shared Jerry's letter with you because I believe it is a very good example of the type of conversations that all of us sometimes have with God in our own minds about whatever it is that we may be dealing with from time to time. Often times we question God then we feel guilty about doing so because of who He is. Most people were probably brought up hearing that one should never question

God. The good news is that God can take it! He wants us to talk to Him. He wants us to be comfortable enough to be able to come to Him with whatever it is that we are feeling. He wants us to have that personal connection with Him, just like we do with our friends. When we talk to God, He listens and He answers. But, we must wait and listen for His voice.

When we take the time to make that personal connection with God, it gives us an opportunity to examine ourselves and our own lives, the choices we make, and whether or not we are doing our part to live our lives the way God intended for us to live. God wants us to live a prosperous life, but who cares what kind of cars we drive, what kind of jobs we have, or how big our houses are. More importantly, do we wake up each morning asking, God how can I please YOU today? Are we as loving and caring as we could be? Are we kind to our neighbors and others, or do we just go about the day selfishly trying to please ourselves? Sometimes having that one on one conversation with God makes us realize how much we have been taking Him for granted. We look around and realize just how blessed we are. And, we also realize how much more we can give of ourselves.

While I sometimes struggle with the guilt of having put my family through grief because of this medical condition, it certainly was comforting for me to experience the tight bond and deep love that we share as a family. We took our faith to the next level, stepped it up a notch in rallying around each other as we continue to pray about everything and to always put God first in everything we do.

The Lady On the Bus

I have a co-worker who is one of only two people with whom I had shared a little bit about my medical condition. Her husband is the pastor of a small church and we would sometimes get into some very heartfelt conversations about God and how good He always is. She would share scriptures with me that definitely helped me get through the tough days at work. She told me a story about a lady she met on the bus one day while on her way home from work. Reading was her favorite thing to do while riding the bus. She was reading *Waiting On God: Fear Is Not An Option* and this very curious lady on the bus started questioning her about the book. My co-worker began to share my story with the lady, explaining everything she knew about the medical condition and how it drew me close to God. Then the lady told my co-worker her story about her own daughter whom, as an infant, had developed a strange bump on her underarm, and she had to have her daughter take some of the same medications that I was taking. It is amazing how whenever we decide to open our mouths and share with others, it always brings about an opportunity for us to learn about others, and suddenly we don't feel so alone anymore.

That lady on the bus said she was amazed at my faith and trust in God. She suggested to my co-worker that I share my story with others in order to bring about awareness of the medical condition. Besides accomplishing that, my greatest hope is to inspire as many people as possible to open their hearts to God and to get to know Him better because only He can fulfill all our needs. I truly believe that God has called me to do His work, to tell people about His mercy and His goodness, and bring them closer to Him. God is the reason I get out of bed every morning. He gives me strength and peace and hope. "And we know that God causes everything to work together for the good of those who love God and are called according to his purpose for them. For God knew his people in advance, and he chose them to become like his Son, so that his Son would be the firstborn among many brothers and sisters. And having chosen them, he called them to come to him. And having called them, he gave them right standing with himself. And having given them right standing, he gave them his glory" (Romans 8:28-30).

Facing Adversity

It is said that adversity is not a dead end, just a detour to a better outcome. Adversity is not the enemy. It is an opportunity. Each one of us experiences adversity during our lifetime. Adversities such as disappointments, sadness, sickness, trials, and heartache are a very difficult part of life, but with God's help, they can lead to spiritual growth, positive change, and progress. Adversity comes from different sources and different kinds of adversity require different responses. As an example, people who are struggling with some sort of illness may simply need to be patient and faithful. Those who are suffering because of the words or actions of others should work toward forgiving those who have offended or hurt them. Or, if your trial is a result of being disobedient, you should be willing to correct the behavior and humbly seek forgiveness. Some adversities are simply just a part of life and can come at any time, whether you are living righteously or not. And sometimes God will use our adversities to teach us lessons that are necessary in His plan for our lives.

Some people, when faced with adversity, complain and become angry. They ask questions like "Why me? Why do I have to suffer like this? What have I done to deserve this?" I was that person during the first few months of my adversity. I was too young to have to deal with such difficulties in my life. Things were going well for me and I was just starting to enjoy my life. So yes, I had a lot of questions. And while these are all fair questions, when we focus on the problem at hand, we can easily put our minds in a state of imprisonment. We not only lose sight of the bigger picture, but we lose all energy and excitement over anything else, and even rob ourselves of any experiences that God may want for us. Besides the intense physical pain I endured, I was miserable, lonely, frustrated, embarrassed, sad, and angry.

Rather than reacting negatively in difficult situations, a more positive approach would prove to be far more beneficial to us. Positive thoughts allow us to think more clearly, which could lead to an earlier resolution in some cases of adversity. It allows us to see the lesson in each experience, which leads to growth and development of character. When we stop being angry at the world for what we are going through, we are able to see others in the same way that God sees them, and we can treat them with a kinder, gentler heart. Most importantly, we fail to remember our many blessings in times of adversity. As much as we would want to believe that no one understands what we are going through, we can take a look around us and see that there are people all around us who are suffering much more than we are.

I was watching a You Tube video about a teenage girl who turned her mom's suicide into an opportunity to help others. Most people would prefer to deal with their adversities in a private way. Small things like getting a bad report card, pimples on the face, or a fight with a best friend are things that teenagers would deal with privately. This young girl used a very painful and tragic situation to create a powerful video, hoping that she could help someone who was suffering in the same way she did. She holds up signs in the video, sharing the story of her mom's suicide and how it has affected her. Despite everything she's been through, she appears very sweet, authentic and caring in the video. She chose to not look sad because she said her mom would want her to be happy. She was always smiling because her mom loved to see her smile. It is amazing how unselfish she is, even though she has been through a heart-wrenching loss. Instead of hanging her head and crying and feeling sorry for herself, she made the video to get across to the viewers her message of hope. She asks the viewers to get help if they are suicidal, or if they know someone who is. She encourages the viewers with a sign that says, "Life gets better."

Once I came to a place of acceptance with my struggles, I recognized that my negative behavior was not helping me in any way. There were some changes that I needed to make. First of all, I started with praying and talking to God. Almost immediately, I began to experience change. My suffering became less burdensome for me, simply because my attitude was finally in alignment with God's ways. I found myself spending more and more time talking to God, not because I felt forced to, but because I saw the difference it was making in my life and I was happier. All my negative feelings and thoughts turned into positive and my self-esteem and confidence were lifted. My scalp started healing remarkably well. I even became bold enough to face my biggest fear, taking my hat off at work and exposing my scars. A famous actress once said, "You can't be brave if you've only had wonderful things happen to you." So it is not the situation, but whether we react negatively or positively to that situation, is what's important. While we cannot always avoid pain, we can choose to suffer less. By faith, I took the first step and called on God and He came through on His promise to always be there when we call on Him.

Why Does God Allow Things To Happen?

It has been asked time and time again, "If God loves us so much, why does he allow bad things to happen to people?" In the Bible, the story of Job is a good example of how Job suffered and God restored Him. Job had it all: a large family, wealth, and blessings of every kind we could ever imagine. This must have bothered Satan because he went to God about it. And God bragged about the blameless and upright man that Job was, a man who feared God and shunned evil. Satan was not convinced about Job's righteousness so he challenged God. Satan told God that Job would curse Him if He were to take away everything from Job that He had blessed Him with. God wanted to prove to Satan that Job was not righteousness just because he was being blessed so He gave Satan control of everything that Job had. Job soon lost everything he had, except his faith in God. Job 1:20-22 tells us that Job reacted like this: "Job stood up and tore his robe in grief. Then he shaved his head and fell to the ground to worship. He said, "I came naked from my mother's womb, and I will be naked when I leave. The Lord gave me what I had, and the Lord has taken it away. Praise the name of the Lord." In all of this, Job did not sin by blaming God.""

Satan must have been very angry at Job's response. Job's suffering seemed unfair, but he did not blame God or ask, "why me?" Job's friends felt bad for him, but they started blaming him for his own troubles, telling him that he must have sinned for all that suffering to come upon him. In the same way, when people see us suffering they unfairly assume that it must be because we have sinned. And sometimes, we are even hard on ourselves, asking, "what have I done wrong to deserve this?" As with Job, suffering is not always as a result of sin. God often uses suffering for the transformation of our character, to get our attention, or for us to become more dependent on Him. So instead of asking, "why me?" or "what have I done wrong?" we should ask, "What is God trying to do?"

When Job's friends started accusing him of sin, Job tried to defend himself against their accusations but his justification quickly turned into self-righteousness and that, in God's eyes, is sin. No man is without sin, and Job was guilty of sin. He became discouraged and began to question God. But God chooses not to tell us everything. He answered Job by saying, "Who is this that questions my wisdom with such ignorant words? Brace yourself like a man, because I have some questions for you, and you must answer them. Where were you when I laid the foundations of the earth? Tell me, if you know so much" (Job 38:2-4). God is involved in everything that goes on in this world and nothing happens that is not within His perfect will. He is never caught off guard or by surprise. His ways are beyond human comprehension and, clearly, He has a purpose when it comes to suffering.

Job never would have questioned God, if he knew that God was going to restore him more than he had in the beginning. "When Job prayed for his friends, the Lord restored his fortunes. In fact, the Lord gave him twice as much as before!" (Job 42:10). God rewarded Job for his faithfulness and his endurance through all his sufferings. So Job ended up much better off than he ever was in the beginning. We all suffer in this life. And while we may not know why, the lesson for us is that God will bless those who are faithful and endure to the end.

I believe there is a reason behind the afflictions that come to us; they don't just happen for any reason. I believe they are within the perfect will of God. He works on us in many ways. He sometimes allows adversities to happen in our lives so we can begin to trust Him. He wants us to get to know Him on a deeper level. So when these situations occur, it is not meant to break us down; it is to strengthen us and build our character. God wants to get us all on His team, and He wants to make non-believers become believers. It doesn't matter what your situation is, or what you are dealing with,

He always shows up at the right time, and reveals Himself when we are at our lowest point.

Through all I have gone through, I have no doubt whatsoever that it was Jesus who pulled me through. I didn't fight the waves of adversity; instead, I rode them. It was very uncomfortable at times, feeling alone and being pulled in the direction of righteousness, while my flesh was fighting with my spirit. My mind raced day and night, tempted by the world and what my friends were doing. I wanted to hang out and party and live my life without restrictions, but I quickly realized that God was trying to get my attention. He wanted to use me for a bigger cause. He gave me the tools I needed, redirected my mind, aligned my thoughts with His, shifted the atmosphere around me, allowing me to touch others through His word.

Where is God When We Need Him?

I read an article not too long ago, where the writer talked about God's purpose behind our problems. He said that as a pastor he often times hears people ask, "Why doesn't God help me in my troubles?" While this is a reasonable question to ask, he said Christians tend to be afraid of asking God why. They think that if they ask why, it would mean that they do not have enough faith, or they do not want others to know, for fear of what people might think of them. However, if we are going through tough times, we need to know why, and what we should do when we are in them. Otherwise, we become confused and frustrated.

What we need to do is adjust the way we perceive life. First of all, bad things do happen and they happen to good people. We will go through trials, troubles, and tribulations, but what we have to do is figure out what we are to do when they happen. What lessons do we learn from them, and how do we grow to become better instead of bitter. Psalm 46:1 says, "God is our refuge and strength, always ready to help in times of trouble." God does not look upon trouble as we do; we see stress, but God sees opportunities. What we see as a crisis, He sees as growth and improvement. God's purpose in times of crisis and trouble is to teach His children precious lessons, to educate us and to build our characters. And when we learn from them and ride out the storms of life, we will see the great promise fulfilled. We need to see the joy and opportunities through times of trouble, because we will learn that there is a sweet and wonderful joy we can have here on earth as well. We do not have to wait until Heaven, we can learn to make our life joy-filled by seizing the crisis and growing from it. We can become the person that we are capable of being for our benefit and His glory.

The writer went on to explain that in the Psalms we see David go through so much, yet he still trust and obey much more than most of us could ever do. And he does this without the New Testament at his disposal, or the scores of resources and places to seek help that we have. David does ask God the hard questions, but he did not stop there. David also knew God intimately and trusted him wholeheartedly even in times of severe trials, and even going through them again and again. According to the Psalms, David had a very strong passion and conviction to God's call.

There Is Always A Lesson

No one likes to go through trials. In fact, we try our hardest to get out of them as quickly as possible and we are thankful when they are over. When it keeps happening and happening, we have got to recognize the crisis as a challenge from God to learn valuable lessons to make us grow in maturity and strength. Perhaps we should look at life as a series of problem solving and learning opportunities, because the problems we face will either overwhelm and overpower us or grow and develop us. Therefore, our joy is determined by how we respond to adversities. Unfortunately, most people, including Christians, fail to see God's hand in their lives. Instead, they choose to focus on the problem and allowing it to take over their lives. When God tests us, or bad stuff happens, our adversities can and will become our tools to grow and learn to be our best for Him. Things that are seemingly against us, He will turn around in His time and way. We have to learn to be still and allow God to work. When it is over, we can look back and see that our trials have been necessary; we become better because of it, and He is glorified!

God wants to use our problems for good, to make us better and stronger for our personal development and in turn for us to be able to help others in their lives. However, an unhappy, confused and frustrated person will react irrationally with their problems rather than taking the time through spiritual discipline to see the advantage they bring them. But there are some things that we can do that will help guide us through the storms of life and get ourselves on the right path.

In the same way that bad weather happens for scientific reasons, the storms in our lives have root causes. Therefore, we must first **determine the reason we are in the storm**. We may need to dig deep below the surface of our fears and experiences to find it. We may have to uncover things we may not want to face, but have to, to be able to get through them. Doing this can prevent a bad decision from being escalated by another and another and so forth. So when the storm clouds begin to form, it is not a time to be impatient and ignore it, hoping it will go away. It is a time to surrender and seek God in prayer, and seek the reason for the storm. In most cases, it is there in plain sight, we just need to get the distractions of fear, our will, and expectations out of the way before we can see it.

The next thing we need to do is **determine what the outcome of the crisis may be.** We should carefully consider the consequences for our decisions and the possibilities for our directions. We need to look ahead and plan accordingly through our prayers and walk with God, because when we have the attitude of learning through it, the storms are not so tough, and we receive the blessing and maturity with less stress and struggle.

The other important thing we need to do is **determine how we are going to respond to the crisis.** We need to ask ourselves what is the best thing we could do. The most beneficial responses would be to deal with the problem, take responsibility for our actions and the part we played in allowing it to happen, and take God's promises to heart. None of these are easy to do, but know that God will give us the strength and perseverance, because what gets us through is not our own strength, but His! We have to be big enough to allow the Holy Spirit to live in us, and we become big by admitting our mistakes and then being willing to correct them. And if we trust and obey God, His love will guide us. Those are some of the building materials He provides us with so our homes can become storm proof. So when the crises come we will ride them out to be better, stronger and more content to be exactly who Christ called us to be!

God will use the problems in our lives to lead us in the right direction. He is always there leading and protecting us, even when we do not see Him. Just as a parent will discipline their child out of love, He will light a fire under us to get us moving if our will is in the way of His will. Without such wakeup calls, we would blindly fall onto the wrong path that would lead to greater disappointment. His love is there to motivate us and change us so we can get on the right path because His plan is better than anything we could ever come up with for ourselves. Our problems will point us in the right direction, if we surrender our will over to His.

Sometimes it takes a painful situation to make us change our ways, and sometimes the only way to learn the lessons of life that will make us better is by suffering and failure. When a parent tells a child not to touch a hot stove, what does the child do? He touches the hot stove! Yes, we learn by being burned. And God is not up in Heaven having fun watching us suffer, but because He loves us so much, He will use our suffering to get our attention. Remember, He sacrificed his own Son and Jesus suffered extreme pain for us. Pain is a part of life, so it is best if we accept and learn from it; however, most people only learn the value of something, such as health, money, or relationships once they have lost it. I remember falling to my knees many, many times, crying my eyes out and praying and begging God to please take away my pain. It was during those trying times that I decided that whatever it was that God was trying to teach me, He got my attention.

Problems can be a blessing in disguise, because they can prevent us from being harmed by something more severe. A good example of being shielded from greater harm is a car breaking down just before it reaches a railroad track while a train is about to zoom by. How we respond and learn when we find ourselves in difficult situations says a lot about our character. God is far more interested in our character than our comfort, and problems are the main ingredients for us to build character; they help us learn to be patient and patience develops strength of character in us and helps us trust God more each time we use it until finally our hope and faith are strong and steady. We will have far more contentment and joy in our lives when we cooperate and allow God's love to rule in our lives, and surrender our fears, desires and pain over to Him.

Our primary goal is to learn from our mistakes and experiences, so we can grow in our faith and practice for God's glory. We can also learn to accept what cannot be changed, and focus on what we still have, not what we have lost. Remember what is important in life. It is not things, not the career, cars, boats, toys, education, looks, power, or status. It is relationships that matter. Focus on God, for He is the secret reservoir of strength that we all have access to. He is who gives us the perseverance in tough times. Place your trust and reliance upon Him, as this is where our stability comes from. Learn to listen to God through prayers and devotions, and listen to Godly advice as this is where our direction comes from.

The Consequences of Fear

Fear is an uncomfortable feeling that we get when something has happened or is going to happen. Despite life's many uncertainties that cause us pain, worry and fear, we are expected to live each day fearlessly; however, we can remain calm and confident knowing that God has promised to help us and strengthen us, and He will always keep His Word. "For God has not given us a spirit of fear and timidity, but of power, love, and self-discipline" (2 Timothy 1:7). Everything good in life comes with a struggle against fear, and we can overcome fear but we must face it with our faith in God that He will give us victory over every area that we have struggled with in the past. "And we know that God causes everything to work together for the good of those who love God and are called according to his purpose for them" (Romans 8:28).

Many times we are afraid of hearing God's voice because we don't want to hear him tell us no. What are we afraid of? Everybody will face the realities of life at some point. All we need to know is God will never reject us. Whether *we* accept *Him* is our decision. He will meet all our needs. If He feeds the birds of the air and clothes the grass with the splendor of lilies, how much more then will He care for us who are made in His image? The only thing we should be concerned with is obeying our heavenly Father and leave all the consequences to Him.

Fear will create doubt and confusion in our lives and affects everyone around us. We can pray and put God first in everything we do, but if we are fearful then our prayers are almost useless. You've probably heard the saying, "If you pray don't worry, and if you're going to worry then don't pray." If we are always afraid, we focus only on our negative thoughts and allow fear to take away our peace. Fear also affects our thinking and actions, causing us to make poor choices, such as turning to destructive habits like drugs and alcohol. Fear will cause us to lose self-confidence and trust in what God can do in our lives, thereby preventing us from becoming the people God wants us to be. In other words, fear will block our spiritual growth if we are afraid to step out in obedience. Courage is not the absence of fear, but it is acting in the face of fear.

Too many of the decisions that we make in our lives are based on fear. We are afraid so we try to avoid the possibility of a crisis. But the truth is that no matter how safe we try to be, tragedy can strike at any time. Living a life based on fear does not make us safe. It paralyzes us and imprisons us. We are afraid to embarrass ourselves, we are afraid that we may not have what it takes, we are afraid to make the wrong decision, we are afraid of failure, but that all means that we could die without having lived our lives. There is no way to know where a path will lead us until we have taken that path. We may think we know. We can make the best decision we can with all of the facts we have but even then, where we end up is usually completely out of our hands. Even with our best intentions, the paths we choose may not always lead us to the expected destination.

Psalm 34:9-10 says, "Fear the Lord, you his godly people, for those who fear him will have all they need. Even strong young lions sometimes go hungry, but those who trust in the Lord will lack no good thing." Sometimes we may become confused when we read the Bible and it tells us how we should feel about God. Fearing the Lord means having a strong degree of reverence for Him. There is a big difference between fear and reverence. Reverence means *respect*; the word fear carries a certain insinuation of terror and intimidation. Adam said, "I heard your voice in the garden, and I was afraid." (Genesis 3:10). Adam heard God's voice and hid in the bushes. That is not the kind of relationship that a loving father wants with his children. He wants them to respect Him, not be of afraid of Him. My earthly father may not have agreed with all of the choices I made growing up, but he loves me and I respect him. As imperfect as our earthly fathers are, if they know how to love us, then how much more is God's love for us? He loves us dearly and if we take the time to understand His love for us, then we can become secure in having a loving relationship with Him. Our background, experiences and circumstances may have influenced where we are in life, but we are responsible for who we become.

So what are we going to do with our fears? We can continue to be fearful and suffer the negative consequences, or we can trust God and place our fears in His hands. Remember, God does not say that He will remove us from fearful circumstances, but He promises to strengthen and sustain us through them. Once we have experienced the goodness of God and how much He loves us, it then becomes our responsibility to honor Him by telling somebody just how good God is.

Many people find it very hard to believe anything unless they can see it. This lack of faith usually comes from the fact that they don't really know what the Bible says. Humbling ourselves and studying and meditating on the Word will help us to focus on God, eliminating our doubts and fears. Therefore, if we seek God, His presence and His love will make it easy for us to have courage and confidence. We can expect to be successful when we are consciously seeking God and doing what He is telling us to do. God says, "Fear not, for I am with you." (Isaiah 43:5). When Peter turned his attention from Jesus and looked to the wind and the waves, he became fearful, lost faith and began to sink. He should never have stopped looking to Jesus.

It is easy to become discouraged, disappointed and impatient with God. Satan uses our moments of physical or emotional weakness to destroy our faith but we must make a decision to be strong and, instead, think of all the times in the past when God showed His faithfulness to us and be thankful. Start having a personal relationship with God through prayer and obedience, and learn to obey the Spirit in the small things. Our doubts and fears will never be fully overcome until we study the Bible, meditate on God's Word and see it for what it is, God's instructions for our lives. I have no doubt that you will be happy you did, then you too will want to tell others about the goodness of God in your life.

The Power of Prayers

How often do we pray for something but we don't really expect God to answer? It is easy to pray casually when we feel discouraged about a situation. But it is important to know that God and his angels are very serious about prayers. Prayer connects us with divine power, and that is definitely a big deal! Prayer has the power to change any situation, even the most challenging ones. Sometimes we pray as if we don't really believe that God will answer us. But no matter how hopeless a situation may seem, God has the power to change it when we pray boldly and expect him to respond. In fact, I believe that God's power is so big that he can do anything. God is always willing to meet us where we are. But if we pray and never expect God to respond, we're placing a limit on what it is that we're inviting Him to do in our lives.

What does the Bible say about prayer? Jesus said to ask. Praying is asking. Matthew 7:7-8 says, "Keep on asking, and you will receive what you ask for. Keep on seeking, and you will find. Keep on knocking, and the door will be opened to you. For everyone who asks, receives; everyone who seeks, finds. And to everyone who knocks, the door will be opened." Prayer can have long lasting results and continuing benefits. The more we pray for ourselves and for others, the stronger our faith becomes. When we pray for the good health and wellbeing of others, those blessings will fall on us as well. We become better people on all levels, physically, emotionally and spiritually. We may not see immediate miraculous results, but in time we can expect to see positive changes. When we pray, it is important to have faith that the prayer will affect our lives and the lives of others. We don't want the words to just fall loosely from our lips but we want to feel them in our hearts. In other words, we should pray with emotion.

When we are faced with adversities we try to do a quick fix ourselves and if that doesn't work, we lean on friends and family to help us out. We might ask a co-worker for help, or perhaps the neighbor offers to lend a hand. Whatever the case may be, we sometimes hear people say, "Well, we've done all we can. The only thing we can do now is pray." If the only thing left to do is pray then it means we've tried everything but prayer and prayer should never be our last resort. However, that was exactly what I was used to doing before I discovered that Jesus is always there, waiting for us to seek Him first. The Lord's Prayer is a model prayer given to us by Jesus to teach us how to pray. And Jesus himself often went off by himself to pray, as an example for us to do the same. "After sending them home, he went up into the hills by himself to pray. Night fell while he was there alone" (Matthew 14:23). If Jesus himself needed to go off and pray, how much more do we need to?

We should never have to feel like praying is a duty. I sometimes would hear people praying and it seems like all they were doing was reciting the same thing over and over, from day to day. Rattling off words with no emotion behind them are to me just dead words. When I pray, I simply talk to Jesus, pour my heart out to Him because I know that He is listening, then I wait and listen for His response, which comes when the Holy Spirit speaks to my heart. Since God is not going to physically come down here and tell me what to do, I move forward in the direction that I am most peaceful with. Praying is very powerful and is so important.

I heard the saying, "Seven days without prayer makes one *weak.*" God is my strength. I hope that you are encouraged to pray with greater faith that God may do something wonderful, and even miraculous things in your life, when you pray. For those who don't believe in the power of prayer, I encourage you to try it for yourselves. You have nothing to lose but everything to gain. Once you are finished praying, let go and trust God to meet you where you are.

Wisdom

The Bible describes wisdom as a good thing, which is learned over time. Proverbs 3:13-18 says, "Joyful is the person who finds wisdom, the one who gains understanding. For wisdom is more profitable than silver, and her wages are better than gold. Wisdom is more precious than rubies; nothing you desire can compare with her. She offers you long life in her right hand, and riches and honor in her left. She will guide you down delightful paths; all her ways are satisfying. Wisdom is a tree of life to those who embrace her; happy are those who hold her tightly."

Most people tend to focus on gaining knowledge, but wisdom is something far more important to be desired. Knowledge and wisdom are somewhat related, yet different in a very important way. Knowledge is a tool, and wisdom is the knowing how to use that tool. In other words, having a hammer and knowing how to use it are two different things. Knowledge is gathered from learning and education, while wisdom is gathered from day to day experiences and is a state of being wise. Knowledge is merely having clarity of facts and truths while wisdom is the practical ability to make consistently good decisions in life. Knowledge is information that we are aware of, and wisdom is the ability to make correct judgments and decisions.

The greatest source of wisdom is the Bible. So why do we need wisdom? It is *wisdom* that allows us the ability to discern between those things we do that are right and wrong. It is wisdom that allows us to have the knowledge and understanding to recognize the right thing to do and having the will and courage to do it. It is wisdom that allows us to understand the consequences of everything we do and say before we act or speak. To please God is to follow the ways of wisdom, which brings us in harmony with God because these ways are in accordance with His will. Having respect for others and living in peace with the people we come in contact with every day are also ways of wisdom that will bring us in harmony God. And let us not forget that when we act with wisdom, it brings us in harmony with ourselves, giving us a sense of joy and inner peace. It feels good to follow our conscience, knowing that we are doing the right thing and avoiding shame and guilt if we were to choose to do wrong. When we try really hard and do our best to act with wisdom, the reward is great. The Bible tells us to pray for wisdom when we don't know what to do. "If you need wisdom, ask our generous God, and he will give it to you . . ." (James 1:5). Praying shows that we are dependent on God, His power and His wisdom.

I Surrender

One would define surrendering to God as giving something over to Him. Whether it is our struggles, desires, or our bad habits, it is true that it definitely involves giving something over to Him; but that's only half of it. Once we give something over to God, we need to replace it with something from Him. When we remove the old stuff, we need to put the new stuff in its place. For example, if we are impatient, when we pray and give our impatient ways over to God we need to also ask Him to bless us with His patience; otherwise, complete surrendering will not take place.

During my most desperate days of struggling with the scalp condition, I prayed so diligently to God, so much more than I ever would have imagined. It felt like there was a war going on between my flesh and my spirit, and there was no peace within me. It seemed like my friends were slowly pulling away as I was hearing from them far less than before. My desire to live the partying lifestyle was slowly slipping away and, soon after, I started feeling a change in my spirit. I felt like God was isolating me from all of my friends. I really missed hanging out with them though so the isolation did not feel good at all. It is a painful process. At the same time, I began to feel like God had a bigger plan for my life, something more than just a healing.

I started having what I believed to be some very serious conversations with God. I told Him I was willing to do whatever I needed to do to please Him. I recognized that God was in control, not me. I had no idea what He was up to, but I was ready to pay attention so I surrendered. It is not something I planned to do just because I needed Him to heal me, but it was necessary if I wanted Him to take control. I believe it is the best decision I have ever made in my life. Not only did my health start to improve, everything else was improving as well: my attitude, patience, relationships, and my understanding of God's Words to name a few. Oh, and favor! I am amazed at how every time I am in the process of doing something, and it could be anything, the outcome is usually better than what I was expecting it to be without me having to do much. That is God's favor! And that is how He operates when you invite Him into your life. He's got my back and I can trust Him! So as I continue to practice my understanding of what it means to surrender to God, I know that I will be faced with challenges, but I believe the blessings will always be greater. It is only once I surrendered my life to God that I started living a purposeful life because it is no longer about me; it's about doing the will of God. And the good news is that anyone can choose to surrender at any time in his or her life—it is never too late!

My Life is Not My Own

"I know, Lord, that our lives are not our own. We are not able to plan our own course" (Jeremiah 10:23). It is obvious that the prophet Jeremiah understands clearly what God wants from us when he was praying. Despite what we may think, we are not free to do as we please and disregard what God wants from us. Jesus paid a price for us when He willingly died on the cross, because of our sinfulness, so that we could have eternal life. Instead of humbling ourselves before God and asking Him what we can do to please Him, we seem to be mostly interested only in what God can do for us. We think life here on earth is only about us, and fulfilling our needs and desires. We want God to bless us because we think we deserve it. We bargain with God and tell him that, if He gives us what we want, then we will serve Him. However, we tend to get that backwards; God does not serve us, we serve Him. Our purpose is to carry out the will of our Father.

According to the first commandment, we are called to love God first. The Bible tells us, "Seek the Kingdom of God above all else, and live righteously, and he will give you everything you need" (Matthew 6:33). This, of course, comes with understanding that God is in control; He is in charge. It is not that God does not want to bless us. He loves all of us and has good plans for us. He wants to bless us. We forget, however, that our lives are not our own. We forget that the gospel message is about what Jesus Christ did for us and how we in turn must love and serve Him for His amazing sacrifice. When we start thinking only in terms of *me* instead of in terms of *Him* we can easily go off track in our walk with God.

When we pray and ask God to bless us with something, say a car or job or a home, we can name it and claim it all we want but if our hearts are not thankful, and if we are not truly delightful in God *first*, then our motives are looked upon as selfish and God will not honor our requests. If we truly want to live the life God intended for us, we must ask the Holy Spirit to change our old ways and bring us new life. And before we start throwing up our hands thinking all this is too hard to do, we must remember that it's not about us. He is worthy of our praise. He wants all the glory. Our job is to recognize that He is in control, not us, and we are to willingly submit ourselves to God's will and His timing. Let us be good managers of all that God has given us and if we are faithful in that, He will give us more. I have learned that the more I let go and let God take control of my life the more I gain, the more freedom I feel, and the more of God's favor I experience.

Hope

Natural hope is a desire, accompanied by the belief that something is obtainable. Bible hope is similar but has a corresponding promise from God. Both natural hope and Bible hope start with a desire, a longing, or a need. For me, hope is not a destination; it is a continuing journey. It is about finding the strength to worship and thank God while we are suffering, in our darkest hour. When it comes to suffering, a normal reaction for most of us is to avoid it at all cost. We either try to run from it, or bargain with God to take it away as quickly as possible. However, when we know that God sometimes allow us to suffer for a purpose, and once we come to a place of acceptance, we can always find hope.

I know you are probably thinking that it is all easier said that done. You are right. It is not easy. In fact, I remember the difficult days when I locked myself in my room and had my own pity parties. I felt very alone, discouraged and miserable. I would think to myself, "I am the one feeling this pain, I am the one having sleepless nights, I am the one feeling isolated, no one else; so don't tell me you understand and don't tell me to have hope because you don't know what this feels like." I wanted to be angry with someone, but whom? In fact, in the beginning, I was angry with God and began to question Him. "Why me?" I asked. I had to seriously talk myself into finding the strength to pray when I did not feel like it, and I started reading the Bible even though it seemed difficult to understand at the time.

We will not find hope in people or things, or in politics or technology or science. And we will not find hope in relationships or accomplishments. This kind of hope is not dependable. It does not always last and it does not mean that a good result is always guaranteed. The reality of life is that many of us have been over-exposed to stress or grief, which causes us to shut down or to abandon all efforts that are aimed at achieving a desired outcome. When this happens, we question our self-confidence and we begin to believe that some goals are simply not within our reach and hope disappears.

The Bible teaches us that we need to put our hope in God. Hope in the Bible means a strong and confident expectation, a supernatural certainty. This kind of hope gives us the strength to go on in life. Hope will start us on a path toward understanding and action. "Such things were written in the Scriptures long ago to teach us. And the Scriptures give us hope and encouragement as we wait patiently for God's promises to be fulfilled" (Romans 15:4).

The more I read the Bible the more I began to experience a special peace in my spirit, and my situation became a little easier for me to cope with each day. So I kept the words of God constantly in mind and in my heart and lived day-by-day knowing that it is the one solid truth in the world that I have to depend on. I found my hope in His Words and began trusting Him. And it is through the struggles of life that hope grows stronger. It does not mean that my life is perfect now. Life is a journey—some days are good and some not so good, but I am sharing with you how I found comfort in God's Words and in my relationship with Him, and you can do the same. "He comforts us in all our troubles so that we can comfort others. When they are troubled, we will be able to give them the same comfort God has given us." (2 Corinthians 1:4).

Forgiveness

The Bible tells us that we must forgive as God forgave us. "Bear with each other and forgive whatever grievances you may have against one another. Forgive as the Lord forgave you" (Colossians 3:13). For most of us, forgiveness does not come easy. How do we forgive when, in most instances, we don't even feel like it? Since God gave us free will, forgiveness is a choice that we make, usually based on our faith and obedience to God and his command to forgive. In order for forgiveness to be complete, we must forgive based on our faith, whether we like it or not, and trust God to do the work in us that needs to be done. It is our job to forgive, by our faith, and it is God's job to do the work of forgiveness in our hearts. It pleases God when we make a commitment to obey and have a desire to please Him.

It is human nature to want to hold a grudge when someone hurts us. In fact, our instinct is to hurt them back. God knows that it is not easy for us to forgive, but it is very important to Him. He intends for us to forgive as many times as is needed, until the matter is settled in our hearts, even if it requires a lifetime of forgiving. "Then Peter came to him and asked, "Lord, how often should I forgive someone who sins against me? Seven times?" "No, not seven times," Jesus replied, "but seventy times seven!" (Matthew 18:21-22). Forgiveness is a very slow process although, once it is complete, there is a freedom that we experience as a result of it. God sets our hearts free from the anger, resentment, bitterness and hurt, when we do forgive.

Prayer is one of the best ways to break down the wall of unforgiveness in our hearts. When we begin to pray for the person who has done us wrong, we start seeing that other person the same way that God sees them. They are precious to Him. And sometimes we come to realize that we are just as much in need of forgiveness as they are. If God forgave us, why can't we forgive another? But because we are full of anger, we sometimes feel like the person we need to forgive should pay for what they did. While it is true that people need to be held accountable for their actions, these people also need us to be patient with them.

God is the only one who can keep the resentment away from us, but that would require us to let go of the belief that we can change the past, or that we can change others. We also need to let go of the belief that we are the ones who can change ourselves. Instead, we need to pray and ask God to take care of the injustices. Once we pray, we must let go and let God do his work. It is not our job to judge the other person. Luke 6:37 says, "Do not judge others, and you will not be judged. Do not condemn others, or it will all come back against you. Forgive others, and you will be forgiven." Each time we forgive, it makes it easier for us the next time we need to forgive. If we practice courage and patience and letting God into the process of forgiveness, it is very similar to exercising a muscle, it only grows stronger and stronger. Casting our burdens onto God is the secret of forgiving. We must trust God and depend on Him instead of ourselves. It is not an easy thing to do, but it can be done. It is the only way we can truly forgive.

Praise Him

Why is praising God important? It is said that praise is the key to powerful living. But often, it is far easier to praise the moonlight than the Creator of the moon. According to the Scriptures, praise is an act of our will that flows out of an awe and reverence for our Creator. Praise gives glory to God and opens us up to a deeper relationship with Him. Praise turns our attention from our problems and on God. We praise Him because He is our Creator, Provider, Healer, Redeemer, Judge, Defender, King of kings, Lord of lords, and much more. As we drawer closer to God, He will draw closer to us. Praise is a powerful spiritual weapon that is guaranteed to work to our benefit while, at the same time, pleasing God.

In the Bible, the book of Psalms gives us hundreds of reasons why praising God is important and those reasons lets us know that praising Him is a good thing. When we read about all of the reasons why we should praise Him, it showcases a list of His wonderful qualities: He is love, full of glory, good, wise, powerful, merciful, faithful, and much more. While it is impossible to list all of the things God has done for us, it is a good exercise to sometimes write down those that come to our minds because it brings our hearts back to Him and helps us to remember how much we owe to Him for saving us, for keeping His promises, for pardoning our sins, for giving us our daily food, and so on. Although many people may choose not to praise God right now, I think of the following scripture and how much it has become a part of my daily life. ". . . That at the name of Jesus every knee should bow, in heaven and on earth and under the earth, and every tongue confess that Jesus Christ is Lord, to the glory of God the Father" (Philippians 2:10-11). Praising God is a very important part of life once we have surrendered to God, because it gives credit where credit is due.

The most important thing to remember is that God *is* worthy of our praise. When we praise God for who He is, we are reminded of His identity and we become more aware of His power in the world and of His presence in our lives. We praise Him for how great He is and we see our own sin and realize our failures as human beings. As we begin to praise God, we set the atmosphere for the time we spend with Him, which reminds us of who it is we are addressing. It allows us to acknowledge whose attention we've gained, focusing on God's works and character and thanking Him for his mercy and grace and forgiveness. It is very easy to forget to praise God for the small miracles in our lives. No matter how small, thanking God for all of His blessings is pleasing to Him. Sometimes we get so caught up in the problems of our daily lives that we have a hard time seeing the positive things going on around us.

We all know what an amazing feeling it is when we receive praise and appreciation from others. Guess what? God loves it too! My dad would always go out of his way to do things for my brothers and me, even though he doesn't have to. He is very mechanically inclined, so when our cars would break down he is always there helping us to figure our what the problem is, and even fixes it himself if he could. He could easily leave us alone to figure things out for ourselves, but helping us whenever he could really saved us hundreds of dollars over time. Mom would always tell us, "Don't forget to thank your dad." We can always assume that when we do something nice for someone they appreciate it, but it is always nice to hear them say it. I am sure dad knows that we appreciate everything he does for us, but personally thanking him and letting him know how much he is appreciated makes him feel good. It also makes me feel good to know that he feels good when he feels appreciated. It is no different with God. He smiles when we express our gratitude to Him. It also brings us joy when we please God by offering praise and thanksgiving to Him. So it is obvious that praise works both ways—we enjoy what is being done for us, and when we express our gratitude to God it brings Him joy.

1Thessalonians 5:16-18 tells us that we are to, "Always be joyful. Never stop praying. Be thankful in all circumstances, for this is God's will for you who belongs to Christ Jesus." And The Lord's Prayer begins with worshipping and praising God. "Our Father which art in heaven, hallowed be thy name. Thy kingdom come. Thy will be done, as in heaven, so in earth" (Luke 11:2). This clearly means that God wants us to praise Him. It does not mean, however, that we are to thank God for the bad things and tragedies that come our way. Before I knew any better I used to say, "I don't know why God gave me this medical condition." But God is not the author of evil and He does not send bad things to happen to us, so He does not want us to receive evil things as though they are from Him. He will, however, use those bad things and turn them around for our good. He wants us to be joyful no matter what is happening in our lives because we have Him, and when we trust Him we will overcome no matter how impossible things may seem. We are to praise God at all times, not just when things go smoothly. We are to bless Him when things go wrong too, even if we don't feel like it. When we constantly grumble and complain about things, it works against us. It puts us, and everyone around us, in a bad mood. When we remain positive, we spread a spirit of joy to others.

I can tell you from experience that keeping an attitude of praise while in the midst of trying times is the most difficult thing to do. I read an article once that said, "Praise is a wonderful method we can use to bring healing and deliverance to our souls and bodies . . ." So I prayed and asked God to give me the strength to remain positive in all my suffering. The more I prayed, the more my faith increased and the more I was able to focus on how I can use my situation to help others. Music also plays an important part in my daily worship. When I listen, I begin to feel God's presence and it immediately lifts my spirit. There are many ways to praise God but no matter how you praise and worship God, it should be about honoring God for His power, love, and grace for all of us!

Don't Miss the Opportunities

Up until a few years ago, I was so caught up in the day-to-day responsibilities of life and my own personal issues that kindness and compassion for others were never in the forefront of my mind. I was a good person, kind and compassionate when I needed to be, but I was too busy trying to figure out how I was going to reward myself after a long week's work. I was busy trying to plan the next party with my friends, so how could I possibly fit anything or anyone else into my schedule. How could I be a blessing to others when I was looking for a blessing for myself?

Once I started my relationship with Jesus, I began to realize that life is no longer about me and my dreams and my problems and my challenges. It is about serving God and living the life He intended for me to live. God wants us to live unselfishly and He wants us to be good and kind and have compassion for others. Today, I'm not just kind and compassionate when I need to be, but I look for ways in which I can give of myself, and my time, whenever I can.

I was driving home from work one night when I saw a woman standing at the freeway exit holding a cardboard sign, as I impatiently waited for the light to change. I had a long and busy day and couldn't wait to get home. Without taking the time to read the sign, I rolled down my window, called her over to my car, gave her two dollars and drove off. No words were exchanged, but I quickly realized that her facial expression was saying something to me. She looked frightened and cold with her hair blowing in the wind and arms folded. There was someone else with her—a friend, sister, cousin, who knows. "I have to go back. They need something else," I thought. I kept on driving but as I pulled into my driveway, glad to be home, I couldn't stop thinking about the two women in the cold night air.

My mom, dad, and brother, Mike, had just finished having dinner when I got home. I told them about the two women at the freeway exit. "I gave them some money, but I have a feeling they need something else so I'm going back to help," I explained. We all put together whatever little cash we had in case they needed it, and Mike offered to go with me just in case I needed his help.

The lady I gave the money to had a huge smile on her face. She was shocked to see me again. "You came back, I can't believe it! Hi, my name is Linda," she said. I introduced myself, and Mike. Linda told us that she and her friend stood out there for over thirty minutes before we arrived. Her car was parked off to the side because they were low on gas and needed coolant. "We just want to get home," she said. "Ok, follow us to the gas station down the street," Mike said. At the gas station, her friend, Teresa, introduced herself and expressed how glad she was that we came to their rescue. With tears in her eyes, Linda told us that earlier a guy wanted her to get in his car so he could take her to a gas station. She felt uncomfortable and said no. "He could have taken me anywhere and kidnapped me. You are my angel," she said. "I'm just glad we could help," I answered. We put the gas and coolant in their car and exchanged phone numbers so they could call and let us know that they made it home safely.

It is common to see people standing at street corners and freeway exits, holding up signs and asking for money but we are always so busy and in a hurry to get to our destination, we often ignore them and keep on going. I have to admit, I too am guilty of that. I didn't take the time to read the sign Linda was holding. I assumed that all they wanted was money so I hurriedly gave what I had and drove off. But something didn't feel right. A little voice spoke to my spirit and told me to go back to help. And even though we never heard from Linda and Teresa again, I'm happy that Mike and I did what felt like the right thing to do that night.

The real joy in life is not in what we get, but in what we give. There is no greater feeling than in making somebody else's day. My goal each day is to do at least one good thing for somebody else. It doesn't have to be something big—whether it is offering a co-worker a ride home when their car is in the shop, buying a friend a cup of coffee, or giving someone a compliment, small acts of kindness are never forgotten. I like to be on the lookout for ways I can be good to people. I've learned that if I bring a smile to someone else's face, God will bring a smile to my face. God intends for us to live our lives not based on how we can be blessed, but how we can be a blessing. When you become someone else's miracle, that is the seed that God will use for your own miracle. I almost missed an opportunity to be a blessing to someone else that night. I hope you are never too busy to recognize the opportunities that come your way for you to be a blessing to others. "Your own soul is nourished when you're kind" (Proverbs 11:17).

The Purpose Behind the Pain

Father Knows Best: An Inspirational Story About Trusting God

As a young girl, Debbie always knew that her father's knowledge and ideas were a whole lot better than hers, so she should have known better than to question her father about anything. Her father had a 'green thumb,' and a knack for anything that can grow in a yard. He kept himself busy, always working with some sort of shrub, vine, or tree.

She tried to build a good relationship with her dad, so one day she decided to spend some quality time with him while he did what he loved to do, working in the garden. She inquired about the plants he tended to and even offered to help. Just as she thought, her dad got excited about the chance to show her a few things and said, "You can help me prune the fruit trees." So she got a large knife and followed him out to the garden. His first instruction was for her to just observe as he showed her how to properly prune a tree.

The healthy looking tree, full of the first signs of spring, suddenly looked lifeless. One by one, her father pruned all the trees, leaving many of the branches that had been completely torn or broken lying on the ground to be collected and burned. She couldn't just observe any longer so she decided to speak up in defense of the next tree. "Dad," she began. "Do you even know what you're doing? These trees look horrible." She would never forget what he said next, how profound it was, and how meaningful it was to his daughter. "To correctly prune the trees, you have to cut off what seems to be good now," he answered. "This is not the best season. If I don't cut these branches off now, the tree will be too full when the fruit should be the best. In fact, the branches will be too heavy and will break themselves. If I simply allow the tree to grow now as it naturally would, I will never get the ripest fruit from the tree when the timing and season is right."

Her father was speaking of things in the physical realm, but her mind and spirit held on tightly to the spiritual analogy he was also speaking of. She let her dad finish and then she quietly made her way back to her car where she cried like she hadn't cried in a long time. She knew she was guilty. That was exactly the way she felt about her own life. The things that seemed to be okay or even good, God seemed to cut away and she then felt like she was left wounded before God. And since she didn't have God's perspective, she always wondered if God knew what He was doing with her. She admitted that sometimes she even got angry and believed God was just out to hurt her.

God always knows what he is doing. And He knows the ripest fruit only comes in the perfect season. Sometimes the things that seem good need to be pruned to make room for the things that are best. "No discipline is enjoyable while it is happening—it's painful! But afterward there will be a peaceful harvest of right living for those who are trained in this way" (Hebrews 12:11).

Whether we believe it or not, there is a purpose behind everything we go through in life. But because we can't physically see God, it is very difficult to see His hands in our lives when we are facing adversity. Deuteronomy 8:2 says, "Remember how the Lord your God led you through the wilderness for these forty years, humbling you and testing you to prove your character, and to find out whether or not you would obey his commands." When we take a closer look at this scripture, we can see that God had a specific purpose for the Children of Israel in the wilderness. He wanted to humble them, test them, and find out whether or not they would obey his commands. The Children of Israel did not do these things. They died in the wilderness because they kept complaining and they never changed. Even though they were *saved* from the hands of Pharaoh and the Egyptians, they died without obtaining God's promised land.

When we are facing adversity, it is expected that we would replace our own ideas and ways with the ways of God otherwise we too can be saved but still miss God's promise. We must be willing to allow God's purpose to work for us in the midst of our adversity. Like the Children of Israel, Jesus himself was in the wilderness, but instead of 40 years, for Him it was only 40 days because He passed every test while He was there! He did not praise Himself because He was the Son of God. He remained humble and did not misuse the power of God that was in Him, and He did not worship another God and sell out for worldly possessions. The Bible tells us that after Jesus came out of the wilderness He began to possess the land. There were signs, wonders and miracles and victory everywhere He went. God wants us to be just like Jesus. He wants us to come out of the wilderness.

Once we have made the decision to live for Christ Jesus, God begins the process of stripping away from us all things that are not Christ-like. In the midst of adversity this process is painful but necessary, and it does not come without the temptations that are designed by Satan to take us off our important path. But when we are obedient God blesses us.

It may not be a bad idea to think of life as a learning experience and each failure is a step toward success. The secret then is to learn from our mistakes. There is a lot of truth in the saying, "The successful man will profit from his mistakes and try again in a different way." We know that doing the same thing over and over again gets us the same results. If we make a slight change each time, the results are going to change. Each time we change the results we are closer to expected success. This is just another way of saying, "If we do what we've done we'll get what we got". So to get different results, try it a different way.

Success comes from innovation. Innovation means a new idea or method. It doesn't mean that we won't ever make mistakes along the way, but being successful simply requires learning from those mistakes and doing things differently. "If life gives you lemons, make lemonade." Without giving this quote much thought, I have been learning how to use every bad situation in my life to my advantage. It seems like every time the stool got kicked out from under me, I always found a way to make things better. I've learned that no matter how bad the situation may seem, there is always a solution. Every bad situation we are faced with could always be worse.

We can take any "lemon" and turn it into lemonade. We just have to be willing to look long and hard enough at the situation to find how it can be turned around to our advantage. For instance, if we lose a job, we can find a new career. If we lose a love relationship, we can always find someone else to love. Almost anything we lose we can find something to replace it with. The key is to not dwell on the "sour lemon" so much so that we cannot think of what we must do to make it into a sweet and refreshing drink. We can be so absorbed in our problems that we are unable to look for the solutions. Instead, we talk to our friends about our problems, we cry to relatives about how unfair life is, and we look for sympathy anywhere we can find it.

When we keep focusing on the problems in our lives, they will tend to manifest themselves even stronger. Our lives are exactly what we focus on. The more we focus on misfortune, the more harm we do to ourselves. When we worry our stress increases, our health deteriorates, and our attitude becomes negative. We should not get so absorbed in our problems that we do not see the challenge they could present for us. We must learn to see a situation for what it is. In the middle of every difficult circumstance lies opportunity. Each lemon that comes our way could be an opportunity knocking, if we would only step back and evaluate what has happened.

It doesn't matter what your experiences are, none of them is a waste of time. Whether they were good, bad, or boring, we can learn something from every experience, even if it means we are to just sit still. A famous author once said, "Nothing is a waste of time if you use the experience wisely." Life is built on continuing experiences. Some are good and others not so good. What we experience becomes a part of who we are. There is nothing good or bad about an experience except how we interpret it. For everyone who likes something or someone, there is someone else who dislikes that same person or thing. Whether you fail or succeed, it doesn't matter if by doing so you've learned something that you can use to your advantage. Even if you strongly dislike a person, that can be used to your advantage if you look at the entire situation and create a positive experience from it. You may learn that hating only hurts you, not the target of your hatred; their life goes on as if you didn't exist. Turning your dislike to a small bit of understanding of that person's circumstance could give you insight into your own life. If a tool gets broken while using it, that teaches you how not to use that tool the next time you may want to use it. A broken friendship gives you strength in building your next friendship. Of course, each of these scenarios is based on "if you use the experience wisely".

We can learn something from everything we do. We also learn from our mistakes. For example, if we do something stupid and feel like it was a waste of time, it wasn't really a waste of time because now we know it was a stupid thing to do and we won't do it again. And if we 'waste our time' on the Internet or something like that, then we will realize that next time we need to spend our time more wisely. So nothing is really a waste because everything we do teaches us something.

Sometimes we do things over and over again and never get the result we are looking for. Often we do the same thing, get the same results and still do it again. Our experiences allow us to recognize a mistake when we make it again. Or, at least we hope we recognize it the second or third time around. Some people make the same mistake over and over again and never learn from them. Many times it seems like we are on a treadmill of experience and we are going nowhere. Our life seems to go in circles and we repeat our mistakes again and again.

Next time we are dealt an unfair hand by life, we should take a look at it carefully and ask *what can I find in the situation that I can make better with a slight attitude adjustment?* Once we find out what it is, make that change then look for another thing and another. Without realizing it, we can find ourselves making lemonade out of lemons. The most important thing though is that we need to always remember God's bigger plan for our lives, even when it looks like we're going through a bunch of stuff that makes no sense at all to us.

How to Find Your Purpose

The dictionary defines *purpose* as the reason for which something exists, or is done or made. It is a goal; an intended or desired result.

God's purpose for our lives is HIS intentions and desires so He can get the glory in the end. Finding God's purpose for our lives can make it much easier for us to get through difficulties in life. Our thoughts are very powerful and how we react to the various situations in our daily lives will definitely affect the outcome of those situations. We can clog our brains and prevent ourselves from thinking clearly when we react negatively. If we walk around each day complaining about feeling sick, having no money, and how much we hate the way our lives are going, then we would constantly be uncomfortable with ourselves. Our purpose is not to focus on the problem at hand, but rather to see the light at the end of the tunnel. We should never think about how big the problem is; instead, we must remember how big our God is. If we can do this, we can learn to trust Him more, and to let go and let God take control of our lives. Each one of us has a purpose for our life—God's purpose.

God knows exactly what He intends for us to become, and He knows exactly what circumstances, both good and bad, are necessary to produce the results He desires for our lives. He never allows too much adversity in our lives, but always just exactly what is enough for us. Remember, the purpose of God's discipline is not to punish us, but to transform us into the likeness of Christ. Usually, when we are being trained in a new profession, or if a coach is teaching sports fundamentals, there is usually an explanation as to why it is that we are doing certain things. So when we know exactly why we are doing something, then it doesn't seem so difficult to endure the training or testing period, and that is because we also know what the end result will be. On the other hand, God never explains to us what He is doing or why and, as human beings, we tend to get impatient and eager because all we are really interested in is the end result and how we benefit from it. Nevertheless, God wants us to remain close to Him and love Him unconditionally, even through the difficult times. And in the midst of adversity, Satan is happily waiting to take control of us. He quickly grasps at the opportunity to whisper negativity against God, such as, "If He loved you he would not have allowed this to happen to you." And while we struggle with our own doubts, we would also be tempted to doubt God's love for us. The temptations are going to be there, but we cannot let the negative thoughts linger in our minds.

So how do we discover our real purpose in life? We are not talking about our jobs, daily responsibilities or long-term goals. We are talking about the real reason why we are here, the very reason we exist. To discover our true purpose we have to first be willing to empty our minds of everything we think our purpose is. It is only then that we can fully focus on finding the answer to the question, "What is my true purpose in life?" Writing down all the answers that come to mind could be very helpful in the process. You may discover several answers that seem like the right one, but when the *true* answer comes the surge of emotion that comes with it is usually what determines that that is your purpose. It doesn't matter if you have been working as a waitress or a teacher or a doctor; when you find your own unique answer to the question of why you are really here, it will touch you deeply. The words will seem to have a special energy to you, and you will feel that energy whenever you read them.

Discovering our purpose is the easy part. Working towards becoming that purpose is the hard part. I truly believe that I have found my purpose: It is to live my life according to the purpose God intended for me, to be obedient to His Words, to serve Him, to tell the world about His goodness, and to encourage others to have a relationship with Him as well.

What is Your Purpose?

Sometimes the battle you are fighting or the problem that is staring you in the face just may be the very thing that could lead you to your purpose. Whatever you are most passionate about could also lead you to your purpose. Remember, money should never be the driving force behind your purpose. Instead, it is that burning sensation and tingling feeling that you get deep down inside to do what you are good at. When you realize what that special thing is, if it is God's purpose for your life, then everything else will fall into place. And when God chooses you, He will also qualify you. If God gives you the vision, He will also give you the provision. So, when we put God first in everything we do, He will direct our paths.

A well-known pastor once explained that many of us have lost our perspective on what the real issue is here on earth. He said that what we don't realize is that we have not been given the opportunity to live, but to accomplish the will of God for our lives. We all have a certain amount of years on earth and we have the option to choose whether or not we want to turn our lives over to God. He said most people though are scared to change because they have been programmed to the worldly system. However, if we were in the spiritual realm and we could see Heaven and Hell we would change within three seconds. And, when we align ourselves with the word of God, He will show us our need to change. Romans 12:1-2 says, "And so, dear brothers and sisters, I plead with you to give your bodies to God because of all he has done for you. Let them be a living and holy sacrifice—the kind he will find acceptable. This is truly the way to worship him. Don't copy the behavior and customs of this world, but let God transform you into a new person by changing the way you think. Then you will learn to know God's will for you, which is good and pleasing and perfect."

The purpose for our lives here on earth is to be molded in the image of the Son of God. The big question is, are we willing to leave our comfort zone and be a little uncomfortable while we arrive at the place of our appointment? When we are certain of our purpose, trouble cannot stand a chance. After all, whatever God has for us holds a future and will bring us utmost fulfillment.

We all have a great destiny waiting to emerge and it's our choice to make it welcome. In quiet moments when we are honest with ourselves we can tune in to the urge, the inner call to be more and never less than our true selves. There is something about each one of us that is uniquely incredible.

Why on earth am I here?

We all must value ourselves enough to ask this very important question and we must learn to take ourselves, and our future seriously. This requires us to first make a commitment, which could be as simple as making sure that we do not settle for anything less than living out our dreams, even if we can't quite recognize what they are right now. If we commit ourselves one hundred percent to knowing what our purpose is, our minds can then go to work, consciously and subconsciously and find the answers. We are brilliant human beings. What we focus on, we find.

Once we make that commitment, we pray and ask God to make it possible for us to reach our fullest potentials. Remember, we cannot pray for something without seeing the rest of our lives in its context. Negative behaviors may begin to surface, along with obvious choices, and we are the only ones on the face of the earth with the capabilities to figure it out. Only you will know if your heart and mind are living out what they were created to be and do.

After praying, we should start asking ourselves questions like: *What would I really love to do? What makes me feel good? What energizes me?* If we ask and are willing to be enlightened, our hearts will speak and we will know. Who we are is waiting to be discovered and expressed.

Many of us have been living from day to day with negative thought patterns. The question we might need to ask at this point is *what would we never do?* The reason we need to ask ourselves that question is that we may have been told by someone in the past that we would never be good enough to do this or that, and that may be the very thing that has always been our passion. So if we are thinking a lot about what we could never do, then it's time to ask why not. There is a reason we still think about it.

Once we have established what we love doing, we should start focusing on what it is about the world that we would want to change. Part of who we are is what we have seen and experienced. Part of who we are is our pain. Not only do we deserve to be doing what we are passionate about, we also deserve to be doing it to make a difference.

Think about it for a second. *What would you like to see different around here? What would make the world a better place for people?* For example, think about how fulfilling or empowering it would be for an abused child to grow up and write books that would educate people on how to recognize and stop abuse!

After figuring out what we love doing and what we want to do to make a difference in the world, it is time to write out our visions. A vision will work best if it's clear and filled with details that inspire. In order to become all we have been created to be, we must be able to see it and meditate on it. A clear vision of our future is necessary to begin the journey of following what we now know to be our purpose. My vision board includes all of the things that I could possibly think of that would allow me to live my life the way God intended it for me. For example, I knew that I wanted Jesus to be the center of my life, so I got one of my favorite pictures of Jesus and put it at the center of my board. Next, I asked God to bless me with a good wife and children, so I found a picture of a family having fun while spending quality time together and I added that to my board, and so forth.

Jesus to the Rescue:
A Story About Finding Purpose Here on Earth

I once heard a story about a young woman who was raised in an alcoholic home so she followed the only path she knew. By age thirteen she was an alcoholic. The disease grew fast and soon took over her life. She experimented with pot, acid, mescaline, crack, cocaine, heroin and every alcoholic drink she could get her hands on. As her life became more and more unmanageable, she lied, stole, and used people to get dope. She didn't realize how bad it was until the day she stole her best friend's food stamps and traded them for dope. By age nineteen, she was alone with two young children, a drinking problem, a drug habit, and no place to live. She felt like the whole world was against her. Her friends did not trust her and she was too ashamed to go around her family. She was mad at God for letting all these things happen to her. "Where was He anyway," she thought. He had abandoned her and everything that could go wrong in her life went wrong. Her parents got a divorce, and all of her brothers and sisters were hooked on drugs and alcohol as well.

For years she struggled with the feeling of not belonging. She was scared and most of the time lived in fear and confusion. She felt hopeless and helpless and tried to commit suicide twice. The only thing she ever wanted was for someone to love her and care about her. But maybe that was too much for her to ask. As her life continued to get worse, her younger sister's life was slowly taking a turn for the better. She had met a young man whose family was Christian and she started going to church with them. They eventually got married and moved right next door to her. Her sister started talking to her about God and told her God loved her just the way she was and that He had a better life for her than the one she was living. She told her that God would help her, if she let Him. She listened, but she had a hard time believing it. Her sister begged and begged her for a long time to go to church with her. She promised she would but then made other plans just to avoid going to church.

One day when she could no longer say no to her sister, she went to the liquor store, bought some beer, drank it and went to church. They were a little bit late, but walked in just in time to hear the preacher say, ". . . and God loves you just the way you are!" She was shocked to hear that, and sank down into her seat and just listened. She didn't remember everything that was said that night, but when it was time for the altar call, she didn't even have to think about it when her brother-in-law asked her if she wanted to go up there. She said yes and he went up with her.

She told how, from that moment on, she knew her life would never be the same. Through God's grace and healing power, she found hope. Everything hasn't been perfect. She still has a long way to go but since accepting Jesus as her Savior, her life has never been as bad as it used to be and she knows it is only going to get better. The difference is she doesn't feel alone anymore. She doesn't have to rely on herself to make things better, and she no longer has to carry any burdens by herself because Jesus will be with her always. She believes that. She has hope that things are really going to be okay. She feels loved and now knows that she does have a purpose here on this earth.

Music has always been a big part of her life. She plays the guitar and writes songs. She is now a Christian, and she wants to lift Jesus up with every song she writes, every note she sings and every testimony she gives. She said that as God continues to gently heal her damaged emotions and restore life to her soul, she can't help but sing about it! God has since called her to full-time ministry. She followed God's leading and is now working full-time with a band in music ministry. She said, "Everywhere we go there are people who need and want to be ministered to. Music has a way of touching hearts and changing lives. Nothing in this world is more important to me than to serve Jesus in the ministry He has called me to."

Hearing God's Voice

It sounds like a very simple thing to do, but as easy as it is for us to speak to God, many Christians have a hard time hearing His voice and this is not what God intended it to be. He wants an intimate relationship with us, and hearing God speak to us personally has to be one of the greatest benefits of having that relationship with Him. Learning to clearly distinguish God's voice is very valuable because instead of going through life blindly, we can have the wisdom of God guide and protect us. Whatever type of crisis we are facing, the Lord knows exactly how to turn that situation around. It's just a matter of hearing His voice.

The Lord is constantly speaking to us and giving us His direction. It is never the Lord who is not speaking, but it is us who are not hearing. In fact, all true believers can and do hear the voice of God; they just don't recognize what they are hearing as being God's voice. I read an article once where the writer explains it best. He said radio and television stations transmit twenty-four hours a day, seven days a week, but we only hear them when we turn the receiver on and tune in to the stations. When we don't hear the signal, it doesn't mean that the station is not transmitting, it just means that the receiver is not on or not tuned in. In that same manner, God is constantly speaking to His children, but few are turned on and tuned in. While in prayer, most Christians continue to plead with God to speak to them when the problem is with their receivers and their tuning. The first thing we need to do is fix our receivers. We must believe that God is already speaking; we just need to start listening. However, that takes time, effort, and focus. On average our lifestyles are so busy, we are not set up so we can hear God's voice. All of us seem to be busier than ever, and that's one of the big reasons we don't hear the voice of the Lord better. We're just too busy.

Psalm 46:10 says, *"Be still, and know that I am God!"* It is in stillness, not busyness, that we tune our spiritual ears to hear the voice of God. The Lord always speaks to us in that "still, small voice," but it is often drowned out in the midst of all the busyness of our daily lives. The voice of the Lord comes to us in our own thoughts, so that is another reason why most of us cannot hear His voice; we always mistake His voice for our own thoughts. Communication with God is spirit to spirit, not brain to brain or mouth to ear, the way we communicate in the physical realm. The Lord speaks to our spirits, not in words, but in thoughts and impressions. Then our spirits speak to us in words. For example, the Lord is not going to physically come to you and say "You do this or that," but He will urge your spirit to do something, and then your spirit says, "I think I should do . . . ." Therefore, we often miss the direction of the Lord, thinking it's our own thoughts.

At one time or another, each one of us has done something stupid and afterwards we just did not feel right about the decision we made. We knew it was the wrong thing to do, but we did it anyway, only to find out that our impression was actually God speaking to us. However, being human, we go along with logic instead of listening to our hearts. And when it is all said and done, we realize that it was the Lord speaking to us, and we had dismissed the feelings and thoughts as our own. We should learn never to ignore what we feel in our hearts.

Psalm 37:4 says, *"Delight thyself also in the Lord; and he shall give thee the desires of thine heart."* Many times this verse has been interpreted to mean that God will give us whatever we want; but what it really means is that if we are seeking God, He will put His wants and desires for our lives into our hearts and they will become our wants and desires. I heard a story once about a man who was excited to go on a trip to another country. As his departure date drew nearer, and as he prayed about it, he lost his desire to go. Instead he started dreading the idea about going on this trip. He wanted to make sure that he was seeking God about the situation because it was rather strange that he was having such a change of heart. However, the more he prayed about it, the more he realized that he really did not want to go and he eventually cancelled the trip. He found out later on that the plane he had booked his flight on crashed on take-off, killing all passengers on board. The Lord was warning him of that and saved his life, not by saying, "Don't go on the trip," but by communicating to his spirit and taking away his desire to go. That is the way the Lord speaks to us, and we often miss that kind of communication.

The key to hearing God's voice is faith. Our gracious heavenly Father constantly speaks to every one of His children, giving us all the information and guidance we need in our daily lives. We must heighten our sensitivity and discernment, and wait before God to hear His voice. We learn God's voice by having a relationship with Him. The more we walk with God, the more we hear His voice; the more we experience God's voice, the more we know it.

The problem is not with His transmitter; it's our receiver that needs help. Most people continuously ask God to speak, when it's our hearing that needs to be adjusted. Having faith that God is speaking and then learning to listen and obey will transform our relationships with the Lord, and it could save our lives just as in the story above.

Being Obedient to His Voice

Jesus loves us and is very concerned about us and He wants us to do more than participate in good works. He wants us to believe in Him. He wants us to be "like" Him. When we are being obedient to God, we are doing just that: knowing Him, loving Him, and having a personal, intimate relationship with Him. To do this, we must be attentive to God's laws. This is not an option, because we can't have an intimate relationship with Jesus and trample on the words He taught. Being obedient to God is not the same as sticking to the speed limit in traffic because we get a fine if we disobey. Obedience to God is taking His Word into our hearts and living by it because we want to and enjoy being filled with the love of Jesus. We must believe in Jesus, we must have faith in Him, and we must trust Him! When we make the transition to become the person who is having a deep personal and intimate relationship with the Lord, then we can have the highest of joys, the deepest of peace, and receive the fullest measure of God's love and power each and every day of our lives. Remember, there is nothing we can do to make Jesus love us more.

How important is obedience to God? Obedience to God is very important in our spiritual growth. In the gospel of John, obedience to God is underscored time and time again. John 14:15 says "If you love me, obey my commandments." And the greatest commandment is to love God by keeping His commandments. Matthew 22:36-38 says, "Teacher, which is the most important commandment in the law of Moses?" Jesus replied, "'You must love the Lord your God with all your heart, all your soul, and all your mind.' This is the first and greatest commandment.'" We can honor and maintain obedience to God by focusing and meditating on the words of Jesus in order to understand it more deeply. Proverbs 14:15 make a good point: "Only simpletons believe anything they're told! The prudent carefully consider their steps."

Obedience to God is simple. We are to do as we are told. It is that simple. To be obedient is to be submissive and willing to obey. To be willing means to obey with joy. To be willing to obey means that we should have already realized what needs to be done and do it without being asked. Our flesh may tell us that it cannot be done, but Matthew 19:26 tells us that with God ALL things are possible. It says ALL, not just some. So, what He does for one He will do for you.

It is a blessing when we are corrected. In our obedience we will be blessed. But, as with all of God's promises, there is a requirement from us. We must obey! It is not as hard as we think. No one enjoyed getting spanked or grounded as a kid, but being an adult and thinking that we no longer need correction is worse. The sinful nature of man is such that we hate correction, but just keep in mind that God only corrects us because He loves us. What child is not disciplined by his father? Our earthly fathers disciplined us for a little while as they thought best; but God disciplines us for our good, that we may share in His holiness. No discipline seems pleasant at the time. Discipline is painful. Later on, however, it produces a harvest of righteousness and peace for those who have been trained by it. So let us rejoice in God's discipline because it means that He loves us. The most important thing, however, is to learn from our discipline and to not repeat our mistakes. If God corrects us, it is for a reason. The Lord does nothing without a reason, and we know that in all things God works for the good of those who love Him, who have been called according to his purpose. God works ALL things for good, even correction.

I read a story once about a woman who always wondered what it actually meant to walk in obedience with God. She worked in the missions and told how it was such a big deal for her when she was asked to attend a three-week conference in Germany. It meant that for the first time in years she would have to fly alone. It also meant leaving her five and two year old children with their dad for that time and she had never been away from her husband for more than ten days.

So, why did she go? She said she wholeheartedly believed that God had asked her to. The assignment both excited her and severely challenged her. As the months went on and she saw the financial provision that would enable her to go she was both excited and at times angry that God would ask her to leave her family behind. She had mixed emotions right up to the night before she left, and she even wanted to question God about why He was asking her to go without her family, but she had to obey.

In terms of other missionaries, she never had to uproot her family or go to a tribal village where there was no church and where she had to learn a new language. But the principle of being obedient is the same no matter where we are. As one of the speakers said at the conference, "even if you are not successful, you must be obedient." For her, part of her going away was simply about being obedient.

She said that looking back, it did not surprise her that God wanted her to go. She believed that He wanted some "me" time with her so that she could fully focus with no distractions. "Following God's call is hard to decipher, and sometimes he places something so much on your heart, it's as if God is shouting through a megaphone," she said. "And whether it is a megaphone or that still small voice, it is important to be obedient. Whether you are successful or not is secondary. It is faithfulness and obedience first. God honors those that honor Him." "Loving God means keeping his commandments, and his commands are not burdensome" (1 John 5:3).

The media shows us many different pictures of what love looks like, but the Bible tells us that love is seen by one thing: obedience. It's not a warm and fuzzy feeling, though love does feel that way at times. It's not about cute little animals and babies, though they make us feel loved. But simply put, love is seen in obedience. For example, if a child says they love their parents but do not obey them, we would have to question their love. If a husband says he loves his wife and does not respect her wishes but does his own thing, we would question his love. So how can we say we love God, if we do not obey Him? Most of the tests of our love for God are in the little things, just like it was for Eve back in the beginning. Eating a little piece of fruit should not be a big deal! But to God it made all the difference, because it's in the little things where true love and obedience are seen. Are you obedient to Him? Or, asked differently, do you love Him?

Make The Most of Wherever You Are

I heard another interesting story about a young woman who heard God's voice and was obedient. She said she clearly remembers sitting on her bed at four years old and asking Jesus to come into her heart and live there. Over the years, the pieces of the puzzle of Christianity began fitting into place as her faith grew. Her family moved to Liberia when she was ten, with frequent periods back in the United States. One of those periods was during her first year of high school. She went to a Christian high school, but was shocked to hear the kids cussing and talking about sleeping around.

It confused her to think that they talked like that but they claimed to be Christians. It was heartbreaking and disappointing for her that they confessed Christ with their mouth, but their actions did not portray Him and she did not want to live that way.

They returned to Africa, and when she was sixteen years old there was a massive coup and they had to evacuate with just the clothes on their backs. Everything was stripped from them. She wanted to believe in her heart that they would go back, but then her father sat her down one day and told her that there was nothing there for them to go back to.

That was a very hard year for her. She felt like she had lost everything. She didn't know anyone and, like many teenagers, she was struggling with hormones and emotions. As she sat at lunch one day, God spoke to her and said, "Make me Lord. Trust me with your life. These circumstances have been allowed by me and are part of the plan for your life. Wherever I put you, I want you to bloom and give off a beautiful fragrance. Don't pout or be upset—make the most of wherever you are because I have a purpose for where I placed you." She said on that day Christ became more than Savior, He became Lord of her life. What a perfect example that story is of how God wants us to trust Him and let Him take control of our lives, and watch everything else fall into place as we live the purposeful lives He intended for us.

God's Favor

We all know that if people gave us preferential treatment, life for us would be better. The dictionary defines favor as to show preferential treatment, to give advantage to another, and to give special favors. It is Christ-like to have favor working in your life. "Jesus grew in wisdom and in stature and in favor with God and all the people" (Luke 2:52). We all want to be like Jesus. To be like Him means that we should also grow in favor with people. Favor has its benefits but you have to put it to work. You have to believe for it.

In the Bible, the best story about favor working in someone's life is the story of Joseph. Everything started off bad with him. He was his father's favorite son but his brothers hated him and sold him as a slave. Despite everything that Joseph went through, he did not let the circumstances get him down. He stayed optimistic. He was generous in forgiveness and he was not resentful or vindictive. Joseph had a big heart. This is why God gave him favor with so many people. He had reasons to become bitter, but he ignored them and chose to forgive people, including his brothers. Favor is not based on luck, but on a big heart.

Having God's favor is having God's blessings on our lives. It does not mean we will never have to struggle with anything, but we believe for good things. It is easy to become frustrated and disappointed when we are going through something, and it is easy to stay in a negative frame of mind, but it benefits us to have positive and grateful attitudes because it is our attitudes and our big hearts that will determine how we live our lives. Every believer has favor to some degree and the more we please God the more we will be favored by Him; however, we should not think of this as some secret formula for getting whatever we want. It is important to understand also that God's favor will more likely come in spiritual blessings more than in material blessings. We should all desire and seek to have favor in the eyes of God. We can grow in that favor as we faithfully live for Him.

Miracles versus Blessings

I read an article recently that was written by a pastor, explaining what the difference is between a miracle and a blessing from God. He said that there is no doubt that God performs miracles and uses them to draw people close to Him; however, God's intent for our lives is that we are able to function under His blessings. Blessings prevent crises, while miracles deliver us from crises. So, if we are living from miracle to miracle, it probably means that we are living from crises to crises. He goes on to draw examples by asking, "Would you rather receive a *miracle* of healing or live with the *blessing* of good health? Would you rather the Lord perform a *miracle* to pull you out of bankruptcy or be so *blessed* financially that He wouldn't have to perform the miracle? The logical answer to both of those questions is obvious. Of course, it is better to avoid problems than it is to be delivered out of them. We all are already blessed but most don't know the power of the blessing; they would rather receive a miracle. The writer explained that we could begin to prosper as never before, if we can make the adjustment from a miracle mentality to a blessing mentality.

If sin did not corrupt God's creation, everyone would be healthy and prosperous and there would be no need for miracles. But with all the corruption here on earth there will always be a place for miracles.

Thankfully, Jesus not only forgave us of our sins, He redeemed us from the curse and placed blessings on us. Another example the pastor gave was, if we abuse our bodies we could receive a miracle of healing; but if the root of the problem is not addressed, the sickness would return and we would need another miracle. But when we believe God's Word and follow its instructions, it will teach us how to eat, exercise, and enjoy emotional health that works like a medicine. The Lord would rather keep you healthy through His blessing than to heal you by a miracle.

Whether we receive a miracle or a blessing from God, we know that God is always taking care of us because he loves us. The only thing that can stop God's blessings in our lives is our unbelief.

Having Faith

Faith is the substance of things hoped for, the evidence of things not seen (Hebrews 11:1). Faith is a necessary part of spiritual discipline. In fact, without it no spiritual discipline can begin. Faith is a very important part of our relationship with God and we must recognize and acknowledge His divine presence in our hearts in order to seek and receive His guidance. Faith is not religion. When people say, "We have our faith," what they really mean is that they have a certain way of doing things that have been passed down from generations; they have their religious ideas and beliefs. And faith is not magical, nor is it a way to get God to do what we want Him to do. To have faith is to believe in something or someone to the point where you fully trust them; you are so confident that you base your actions on what you believe. Faith in God must be from the heart. It is not just intellectual; it is spiritual. Faith causes you to know in your heart before you see with your eyes. "For we walk by faith, not by sight." (2Cor 5.7)

When a child holds high the promise of a father who has never deceived him, and acts as though that promise is true, his faith to him is a base of certainty and of action, and he will act as if these things were so. In the same manner, to have faith in God means we believe what God says. We have never seen heaven; we have never seen an angel; we have never seen God; we have never seen a body raised from the grave, but God has spoken on these subjects and His Word to us is satisfactory evidence, more convincing proof than anything else would be. Human faith is limited to the five senses; it can only believe what it can see, smell, taste, hear or feel. For example, it takes human faith to trust a doctor even if we don't know him; we simply believe everything will be okay. Human faith was given to every person, but in order to believe in something invisible we need God's supernatural faith. Jesus said, "Therefore I say to you, whatever things you ask when you pray, believe that you receive them, and you will have them." (Mark 11:24). This is the kind of supernatural faith that God expects us to have. He wants us to believe that He is responding the very moment we make our requests known to Him. The answer will come, as long as we are patient.

Without faith we cannot please God. In fact, if we don't believe in Him we will not even try to please Him. But having faith in Christ Jesus will lead us to do good works. It will make us want to follow Him and do the good works that He did, such as helping those who are poor and in need, visiting the lonely, caring for the sick, and showing love to all of God's people. And our faith grows and becomes an active force in our lives as we follow His examples and live according to His Word. Faith is not just a declaration of our belief, it is a source of power that can be renewed each day by studying His Word and trying harder to follow His examples.

Everything the Lord does for us is accessed through faith. We have all been given the same measure of faith; however, none of us use all of the faith we have been given. The more we know about faith and how it works, the better it will work for us. Just knowing that we have the same faith Jesus has should take away any hopelessness and motivate us. Eventually, if we just keep trying, we would see results; but most of us are quick to give up because we believe we don't have what it takes. That is not true because God has given us everything we need, including all the faith we need. A lack of faith always leads to a lack of obedience. A man will never really do what God says, if he does not have confidence in God's promises.

It doesn't mean that because we have faith we will not be tested. We can expect difficulties as well as blessings. Faith brings answers to our prayers, and it brings salvation and all the benefits of salvation into our lives, including healing, prosperity, peace, love, joy and all other benefits, which the word of God promises to us. We may not feel full of faith today, but that doesn't mean it has to be that way for the rest of our lives. One way to help us develop our faith is to listen to the Word of God as much as possible. "Faith comes by hearing, and hearing by the Word of God" (Romans 10:17). What we listen to affects what we believe, therefore constant attention to the Word of God produces faith, if we listen with an open heart and an open mind. Remember, each one of us has been given a measure of faith by God; we just have to use and develop it by putting it into action.

Praise and worship and giving thanks to God for the results of our prayers, before we see it, is an act of faith and helps our faith to grow. We also want to believe God for others to be blessed, in a spirit of love, because faith works by love and, as we give of ourselves God will give blessings to us as well.

Acting in Faith

In the Bible, all those who are commended for having great faith did something to express their faith. In John 9:7 Jesus told the blind man to go to the pool and wash and before he received any kind of healing, the blind man acted in obedience to Jesus' words. He was healed because he demonstrated the kind of faith that God required him to have in that situation. He would not have been healed if he had not obeyed. In James 2:20-24 God told Abraham to offer his son Isaac as a sacrifice and Abraham obeyed. Real faith hears the word and the voice of God and acts in obedience, trusting God without a doubt.

I've heard my dad tell the story of his faith over and over again. One night back in 1980, he sat alone in the living room, drinking a beer and smoking a cigarette while trying to relax and unwind after a hard day's work. My mom and brothers had already gone to bed. Dad was changing channels on the TV, searching for something to watch, when the TBN channel caught his attention.

The pastor was talking about faith and healing and about having a personal relationship with Jesus. Before closing, the pastor wanted to pray for the people in the audience and for those watching on TV. As he was praying he said, "Jesus is healing right now. If you want to be healed, and if you have faith, come now. For those of you watching me on TV, I am putting my hand up to the screen; if you want to be healed, come and touch the palm of my hand with the palm of your hand." He said, "You young man, sitting on that couch in your living room, drinking that beer and smoking that cigarette, if you want to quit smoking, and if you have faith, come, touch the screen now." Dad looked around in disbelief—the pastor was talking to him! It felt like the pastor was seeing him right through the TV screen and talking directly to him, he said. Without hesitation, he jumped up and rushed over to the TV, touched the screen with the palm of his hand touching the pastor's hand, while the pastor continued to pray.

Dad said he *immediately* felt his desire for the cigarette and beer disappear while praying. He threw away the cigarettes (a brand new pack he had just opened) and lighter. The next morning he told mom that he quit smoking and showed her the cigarettes and lighter in the trash. She laughed because it looked like he had placed it there in such a way that he could easily pull it out, if he changed his mind.

He told her about the *Jesus* experience he had while she was asleep. She told him he should have given away the cigarettes and lighter to someone who smoked, instead of throwing them away and wasting money. Dad replied, "No, because if it is not good for me, it is not good for anyone else." He said he had tried many, many times on his own to break the addiction of cigarettes, but he always went back to the old habit. That night, he exercised his faith and made a decision to try Jesus and a miracle happened. It's been 33 years since his last cigarette! I am very proud of my dad. I will never get tired of listening to him tell how God healed him from his addiction because each time I hear it, my own faith increases.

While it is possible to have actions without real faith, those actions would be considered dead works. God's Spirit will speak to us through our consciences to lead us to do things based on God's Word. We don't have to have astonishing faith to begin with. We can start small. Even if faith begins as a tiny seed, that is enough to begin with. Over time, and with experience, that tiny seed of faith will surely grow.

The Power of Words

The words we speak showcase the power of the tongue. Every word that comes out of our mouths can have a very powerful effect, good or bad, on our environment. We express faith and fears through words. Promises are established through words. We allow bad spirits to work when we speak bad words, but God and His angels go to work when we speak good words. Words are considered spiritual seeds so it is very important that we are always careful with what we say. To produce love, we must use words of love. To produce faith, we must use words of faith. To produce life and hope, we must speak words of life and hope. In the same manner, words of fear will attract the spirit of fear. That is why the more we study and say God's Word, instead of negative things, the more we will believe it, and the more we believe it, the more we will say it.

When we hear a powerful positive statement it can change our whole mood. Positive words can change how we think about certain things even if we had a negative view of it before. Positive words have power. They have the power to transform us. You've probably heard the saying, "If you can't say anything nice, don't say anything at all." This does not mean that we can never say anything negative. Sometimes it is necessary to talk about something that is negative, but it should not be said in a criticizing way. Rather, it should be done in a positive and uplifting way that will help the other person learn or improve.

Sometimes it can be very difficult to be consistently positive as we may still have doubt in our minds about what God can do for us. However, we can renew our minds by meditating, listening and studying the Word so that we can accept God's principles and promises without any doubt. When the Word is deeply rooted within us, it will change the way we speak, the way we act, and the way we handle difficulties and life's challenges.

It Doesn't Matter

When I was struggling to get through each day at work, suffering with excruciating pain, frustration, embarrassment and disappointment, the only thing I could think of was, "How can I make this suffering go away?" I just wanted my head back the way it was. People were always telling me to "just pray" or "don't stop praying." I also heard a lot of "just keeping praising God." I couldn't understand how I was expected to praise and worship God when I was feeling lousy all the time. I didn't know what to say if I wanted to pray, and I didn't feel like praising God while I was suffering. What was I suppose to praise Him for anyway? I just wanted to be well again. I told myself, "Once I am well again I will be happy to praise God; now is just not a good time." It was not like me to make myself pray and praise God. He gave us free will, so He is not going to force us to do anything. We have choices and He allows us to make our own decisions.

The longer I grumbled and complained about what I was going through, the worse things seemed to get. When I started feeling like we had come to a roadblock and didn't know what else to do, without even thinking about it, I started falling on my knees and having small talks with God. I told God He was all I had left. I would cry uncontrollably while I begged Him to please help me. I was finally ready to invite Him into my life. Immediately, change began to take place. Suddenly, there was a peace within me that I had not experienced before I started praying. That felt good and it seemed like a good place to start to renew my mind. Little by little, the more one on one time I spent with God, the better I felt about myself. Then I started reading the Bible, at first, not because

I wanted to or because I enjoyed it, but because I was asking God for a healing and I felt like one way I could honor Him was to read His book and do my best to obey His instructions for my life. So I prayed and read the Bible with an open mind. To my surprise, the Bible didn't seem as hard to read as when I was younger and my parents forced me to read it. And when I prayed, I talked to God as if I was talking to my brother or a friend, telling Him exactly how I was feeling and what I needed.

It doesn't matter that I don't know the Bible from cover to cover. It doesn't matter that I made Him my last resort and didn't put Him first. It doesn't matter that I didn't feel like singing praises to Him when I was frustrated and things weren't going well. It doesn't matter that I didn't go to church every Sunday. It doesn't matter that I was sometimes impatient and selfish. None of these things matter to Jesus and He did not remind me about any of it. Once I made the decision to ask Jesus to come into my life, He welcomed me with open arms. He immediately revealed His presence—He gave me the peace I needed. In fact, I realized that He had been there all along, working behind the scenes, just waiting for my invitation because He won't force Himself on us. People sometimes make spiritual things a lot more complicated than God intended them to be. However, Jesus gave a promise for everyone to claim by simple faith. I took a step of faith when I invited Jesus into my life.

Although many people may think that they need to clean up their lives before they can be acceptable to God, there is actually nothing we can do to make ourselves more acceptable to God. There is nothing we can do to make Him love us anymore than He already does. While we are expected to change from our sinful ways, it is not something that we have to do before we can come to God. He accepts us just the way we are because we need His help to clean ourselves up. He will begin to change us as we submit ourselves to Him and obey Him. When we hear the saying, "Come as you are," it simply means that God is more concerned with our hearts than our outward appearance and that is the attitude we are expected to have too. It doesn't mean though that we should be careless about the way we look when coming before God. If we can make ourselves look good for weddings and parties, we can certainly do the same for a special occasion like going to church to worship.

When Jesus Shows Up!

I heard a very funny story about a young lady who went to an ice cream shop in Beverly Hills, California to buy an ice cream cone. She was completely shocked when a famous movie star walked in and stood in line right behind her. She could barely keep her composure but she managed to pay for her ice cream cone and left. Once she was outside the shop, she realized she did not have her ice cream cone. She didn't want to look foolish, so she waited outside for a few minutes before going back in. Her ice cream cone was not on the counter and nowhere to be found. She went into deep thought trying to figure out where it could be. A tap on her shoulder interrupted her thoughts. She turned around and found herself face to face with the movie star who suggested that if she was looking for her ice cream cone, she should look in her purse. When the movie star showed up, he had an amazing impact on her. In fact, that's what happens when famous people show up; they tend to have an impact on us. What about Jesus? When Jesus shows up, He has an even bigger impact on our lives.

In *Waiting on God: Fear is Not An Option* I talked about the pastor of a small church who is also a very good friend of my family. In fact, she and my mom had been friends before I was born and over the years my family would visit her church from time to time. During my ordeal with the scalp condition, Pastor Velvia Mosby and her congregation had been offering special prayers on my behalf for a healing. One day Pastor Mosby said to me, "I am inviting you to come *every* Sunday for a few weeks so we can pray for you. We're going to fight this thing together so I need you to be consistent; we need a breakthrough." That was an offer I was not about to turn down. I need all the prayers I could get. So Sunday after Sunday, I would go for prayer. She prayed for me like no one has ever prayed for me before. She prayed for me like I was her own son. I am not going to lie, some Sundays I do not want to get out of bed but I know I need to be there, because Jesus always shows up for me and I look forward to getting lost in His presence when I am there.

My attendance at Miraculous Ministries has gone far beyond just a few weeks. There has been a major transformation within me and my faith has increased tremendously. Pastor Mosby has really taught me how to press into the Word of God. I have always had a relationship with God but with the help of the pastor and her congregation, I feel a spiritual connection that I cannot explain. The presence of God fills the room when she preaches and I get filled with the Holy Spirit. Her teachings of the Word of God are so clear that anyone can grasp it and apply it to their daily lives. It is very obvious that she cares deeply for her congregation. As she prays, she becomes in tune with the spirit as it relates to the individuals present. She gets excited seeing the people draw closer to God, believing, trusting and praising Him more. The entire congregation is just an amazing group of people. I am truly impacted by the personal anointing I receive when I am at Miraculous Ministries, and I am very grateful to be a part of this ministry. I believe I am right where I belong, right where God wants me to be.

This has been the start of a beautiful relationship for me. I like to think of Sunday services at Miraculous Ministries as sessions for the renewing of my spirit, mind and body. A transformation has happened spiritually, mentally and physically. God's desires for my life are becoming my desires, and pleasing Him has become my priority. My mind has become more alert and a spirit inside of me has awakened. I am now a kinder and gentler me. I feel energized physically, and my scalp just keeps improving. Jesus shows up when we invite Him, because He cares. He understands our struggles, and He shows up when things seem hopeless. Everything is different when Jesus shows up. He brings us peace, joy, a new perspective and a new purpose. He fills us with the Holy Spirit, which dwells in us, giving us power over our weaknesses and helping us with our struggles. Without the Holy Spirit, we don't have the power within ourselves to live the life God intended for us to live.

In an effort to honor God, I began looking for ways in which I could give of myself and my time to help to meet the needs of others, so I've recently joined a men's group who works with high school boys to help them to find their passion in life, and to help them maintain a positive attitude as they prepare to live a purposeful life in the world that awaits them. I've also joined forces with a charity that is committed to helping people in our community who are less fortunate. So every other Saturday morning we head out to a Downtown Los Angeles area with food and clothes for the homeless people.

Closing Thoughts

As my journey continues, I hope that you are encouraged to live your best life possible. The only way to do that is to rely on God. Sometimes we rely too much on people instead of relying on God. At some point people will fall short but our Almighty God can give us everything we need. It is not easy to have to go through each day facing adversities. And it may seem like you are at a disadvantage but don't let those thoughts defeat you. Instead of getting depressed and sitting around thinking of all the reasons you can feel sorry for yourself, pray, believe and continue to be your best. Any frustration you may feel going to church every Sunday, praying, praising and shouting for God will slowly go away as you begin to see God moving in the midst of your adversity and your persistence. God never promised that life would be fair, but He did promise that if we trust Him and believe in Him, He would take what is meant for our harm and use it to our advantage. He will fight your battles and He will move you to the next level.

What you are going through may be painful and it may not be right but you have to be able to look forward to what God has next for you. I was weak and helpless and I called on God. I surrendered and told God to use me however He wants to. I told Him that I am the man for the job. I told Him if He will help me, I could do it. If He will strengthen me, I could do it. If you have the right attitude and are willing to take the hands that you have been dealt and make the most of it, you too can do it. It is important to know though that nothing you've been through should keep you from becoming all that God has created you to be. *Philippians 4:13 says, "For I can do everything through Christ, who gives me strength."* God is not going to force us to do anything. He waits on us, and He begins to move in our lives when we are ready for Him to do so. There is a saying that goes like this: "You can be pitiful or you can be powerful but you cannot be both." I know exactly which one I want to be!

Many people believe that before they can have a relationship with God they have to clean up their act and get everything in order before He will accept them. That is not true. I was young and liked to have fun. Partying on the weekends was my way of relaxing after a long and busy week at work. I was just a regular young man who was enjoying life when, out of nowhere, something happened that I could not fix on my own and I needed help. I needed the kind of help that no one but Jesus could give. So I showed up at Jesus' door, just the way I was, and He accepted me. You see, it doesn't matter to Jesus who you are, where you've been, who you know, or what you're going through. He knows our weaknesses and our struggles and He welcomes us with open arms when we come to Him.

I am not a preacher, teacher nor spiritual advisor. I don't profess to know the Bible from cover to cover, and I may not have all the answers to every question. I am still a work in progress, but I do know that I found peace in knowing Jesus. My spirit, mind and body are renewed. I was brought up with a Christian background, so the foundation was there; but I did not like to read the Bible, I did not like to pray, and I did not like going to church. My parents pretty much had to force me to do these things. But I am very grateful to them for having done that because I at least had the sense enough to fall to my knees in prayer when I didn't know what else to do. Yes, it was a difficult situation that brought me to Him but it doesn't have to be that way with you. You don't have to wait for a crisis in your life before getting to know Jesus; you can start having a relationship with Him now.

To all the teens and young adults out there who may be thinking that having a relationship with God means that you will no longer be able to have fun and life will be boring, I am here to tell you that it has been just the opposite for me. I am still the same person who loves to have fun. Some of my desires have changed so I no longer enjoy some of the things I used do, but I am much happier now than I ever was. When God takes away the things from our lives that are not Christ-like He replaces them with new things. I would much rather live my life knowing that I am pleasing God, which is what He intended for us, than living a life of misery and not pleasing Him. One of my favorite TV pastor sums it up like this: "We can either obey God and watch what He does in our lives, or we can disobey Him and wonder what He would have done if we had obeyed Him.

Author Biography

Life's not fair. We live in a fallen world. If life were fair, there would be no sick, poor or orphaned people . . . but like I said, life's not fair.

However, life IS a gift—one to be cherished. Where everyone starts equally: with the sunshine, rain, soil, wind and God. While some may have more and some less of many of those resources, we all have the same amount of God.

Jason Henry comes from an immigrant family, who emigrated from Belize in 1979. The 70's were not friendly to minorities, so they adjusted to their new home, depending on God and being rewarded for their faithfulness.

The Henry family was blessed with four children: Jerry, Howard, Mike, and the youngest being Jason. His brothers were pulled toward the music industry and Jason followed. In pursuit of a career in music, Jason co-produced music alongside his brother Mike for Samuel L. Jackson's movie, Coach Carter, and has worked with world renowned R&B group Boyz II Men and singer Lloyd. Yes . . . success seemed imminent; but like I said . . . life's not fair.

"Many people believe in God as some higher power not interested in the minutia of our daily lives. So we go about pursuing our goals and paying no attention to the fact life goes on—it does not end here. When that day comes, will you regret your choices or be filled with joy?"